HOUSE OF S

HOUSE OF SHATTERING LIGHT

THE LIFE & TEACHINGS
OF A NATIVE AMERICAN MYSTIC

BY JOSEPH RAEL

{*Beautiful Painted Arrow*}

POINTER OAK

Pointer Oak / Tri S Foundation
Distributed by Millichap Books
millichapbooks.com

Edited by Sally Dennison, Carol Haralson and Charlotte Stewart
Interior design by Carol Haralson
Cover design by Source Publications

Printed in the USA

Paperback ISBN 978-0-9823274-4-9
Ebook ISBN 978-0-9823274-5-6

I HAVE LEARNED THERE IS ONLY ONE ACTOR IN THE COSMOS,

AND THAT ACTOR IS CREATING BILLIONS AND BILLIONS OF

RESONATING IMAGES THAT CONTINUALLY MANIFEST AND RETURN

TO THE ONE. SOUND IS THE SOUL OF THE ONE .... THIS

HOUSE OF SHATTERING LIGHT — THIS PERCEPTUAL REALITY IN

WHICH WE LIVE AND OF WHICH WE ARE A PART — EXISTS ONLY

FOR THE SOUL'S CONTINUING.

— JOSEPH RAEL

CONTENTS

HOUSE OF SHATTERING LIGHT

I. THE HOUSE AT LA BOCA

Birthplace

MY NAME IS JOSEPH RAEL. I am an American Indian of Southern Ute and Picuris descent.

You can still see the footings of the house where I was born in a patch of sagebrush desert on the Southern Ute Indian Reservation near La Boca, Colorado, south of Durango. Now there's a two-lane blacktop road near where the house was, and a broken-down corral, its weathered wooden posts leaning in all directions. That was our sheep pen, and just beyond, up the hill, is where we pastured the sheep. When I was five years old I had a vision there.

It was a day in the summer after my fifth birthday, and my mother had sent me to bring back a stray sheep. It was late and the sun was setting when suddenly I noticed that I could not see my mother anywhere. My fears rose quickly to the point where I sought stillness as a refuge, and so I slowly squatted for protection.

I could hear my mother calling from an alternate reality, but I could not see her. In the struggle between the instinct to protect myself by not moving and the urge to run toward my mother's voice, I experienced one of my first visions. A cool sensation came over my physical body, followed soon by a warm stillness, like the feeling of being in my mother's womb. When the warmth came over me I knew it was all right to get up from behind the tall sage.

But when I stood up there was mist everywhere, a white cloud, so I couldn't see where my mother's voice was coming from. All I heard was the sound of her calling my name from somewhere below. When I looked in the direction of her voice and concentrated, a light came from my eyes and made a hole in the cloud-like mist, so that I could see my mother on the other side. I stepped through that hole and ran down the hill to her. Her eyes looked frightened as I reappeared in her world from behind the veil. She pulled me behind her in the direction of home, and through her firmly clasping hand I received pictures of me lying injured in an arroyo.

That evening my mother spoke to my father as she ladled our supper into a bowl on the kitchen table. She said, "I was afraid I would find Earl lying in some deep arroyo out there." (Earl was the name given to me at Taylor Hospital in Ignacio, Colorado, where we went after my birth, and my mother used to call me by it.)

There is a fold in the land on that hillside where one sparsely wooded hill disappears behind another. The desert rises sharply from the road, the hills are rugged and rocky, and clumps of bushes lend a tinge of dusty green to the brown hue of the earth. South of the sheep pen, at a level place in the hillside about fifty feet from the road, our house once stood. No trail leads to it. The last time I visited the place of my birth I had to climb up through the brush. As I crossed a cattle guard, I saw a wayside memorial — a white cross decorated with brightly colored paper flowers, ribbons, and a plastic skull. A family of three had died there the previous year. Their car was said to have spun wildly off the road in a drunk-driving accident. It flipped over and came to rest right there, six feet off the road, in front of what used to be our house, among the mesquite.

The footings of our house are still there, the outlines of a rectangular structure in weathered cement, enclosing a twelve-by fifteen-foot patch of the desert full of cactus and dirt-gray sand. It looks very small now, but six of us once lived there, my father, my mother, my two sisters, my brother, and me.

A few signs of our lives remain — bits of rusted metal, half buried, something that once was a pan, and one heavy rectangle of black rust which used to be part of our stove.

I was born in the bedroom of that house. The last time I visited there, a prickly pear was growing in the very spot where I was born.

In my early childhood, the road was a rutted dirt trail, passable only to a team and wagon during the muddy season. My uncle's Model T was always getting stuck there in the road and we'd have to pull it out. Now this road is a paved highway but is still not used by many cars.

Across the highway is the broad valley leading down to the Pine River. Once, this was all my mother's land. Mother was the granddaughter of a chief of the Southern Ute band. After an earlier marriage which ended in divorce, she married my father, a Tiwa-speaking man from Picuris Pueblo in Northern New Mexico. My half brother and half sister by that earlier marriage had both been sent away to Indian boarding schools by the time I was born in 1935.

From the east side of the road, the desert stretches out flat, then gently slopes downward toward distant trees that mark the river. On the other side of the river, hills roll upward toward mountains on the eastern horizon.

About fifteen feet from the edge of the highway and parallel to it runs a ribbon of vegetation growing from pale soil. That was the railroad track, gone now. It happens to be directly across the road from the cattle guard, where the family of three died in the overturned car.

Here, over half a century ago, when I was six, I showed my two sisters, Corleen and Gloria, then seven and eight, how to kneel down and place their ears on the cool steel of the railroad track to feel the vibrations of a coming train.

Now I wonder if there's something about this place — a crack in material reality, perhaps, where living people are prone to slip through, unawares, into nonmaterial reality. Despite its beauty, this is a dangerous spot.

I have no other way to explain what happened that day in 1940. I remember the excitement of metal humming against our cheeks. Our skin alive with feeling, our eyes wide with wonder, we were mesmerized by it. The vibration of the coming train was so exciting we lost all fear, all sense of time elapsing, all sense to look up and see the train itself. For some reason we all stayed there, ears pressed to the rail, until the train was upon us, and it was too late to move. The same onrushing motion that threw me clear of the churning steel wheels sucked my two sisters under, killing them both instantly.

++++

I can still feel the vibrations of my vanished sisters, the vanished tracks, the vanished house, the vanished lives of my people, among the cactus on Ute Indian lands, and the vanishing Ute language we spoke there, barely remembered today by anyone, even me. I have pressed my ears to all these forms before their dying, to sound the mysteries they embodied on the earth.

I have learned there is only one actor in the cosmos, and that actor is creating billions and billions of resonating images that continually manifest and return to the One. Sound is the soul of the One who drinks the light that It is creating moment by moment in order to continue existence. This House of Shattering Light — this perceptual reality in which we live and of which we are a part — exists only for the soul's continuing.

Now it is time for death's illusion to give way, along with the illusion of material form, before the reality of these vibrations. I believe that if we all learn to listen, the vibrations will give forth their meanings, encoded in the crystal soil of our native earth, to fill the close-pressed ear with song.

Learning to Listen

IT HAS ALWAYS BEEN the Native American way to bond energetically with things rather than to work against them. In order to do this, we have to listen to their vibrations with our whole bodies.

Perhaps my listening started before I was born, before I even had a body. I remember flying, coming very fast up to the house at La Boca, and circling. I was like wind, and maybe not even wind. I came flying into the house where my mother and father and brothers and sisters lived. Some force was pulling me to these people, this house.

It was in winter. I floated in through the walls of the little house and wandered the rooms. I heard my mother complaining about relatives who borrow garden tools and forget to return them. The memory ends there. The next time I arrived, I was in her womb. I couldn't hear her speaking, but her thoughts became like words for me, and these thoughts were the first of many gifts she gave me.

All these impressions from before and just after my birth came to me later in childhood as recurring images. I wasn't sure what they were — why, for instance, my thoughts would take me into the garden where my mother was chasing crows. Chasing the crows from the planted furrows was fun for me when I was in her womb, because they cawed to her as she ran them off. I could experience them through her thoughts.

A few years later, when I was a small child, I would go to my mother's garden in the wintertime, and although no crows were there I could see them. Such images kept returning, and I finally realized as I got older, maybe twelve or thirteen, that the experiences I remembered were not actually mine, but those of another person. Then I realized that they were my mother's experiences transferred to me through her body.

Planting her garden was a pleasing experience for me in her womb because I could become the energies of the plants she loved so well. I knew the physical size of plants in the garden as well as what they were feeling. I had no concepts yet on which to base my perceptions. I was just listening randomly, experiencing the essences of things. Turnips were different from carrots in that they protested loudly for more growing room, and I think Mother heard them because she always planted them properly along the furrows. I perceived the energies of things around us. I knew when my older sister and brother were near because they generated a vitality I could feel in my body when they entered the room.

During the 1960s when we were training Vista volunteers at Picuris Pueblo, we would have them sit with the elders without speaking so that they could simply feel the energy of the elders through their bodies. That way they could get the rhythm, the syntax, the flow of that energy. Energy, when it's transmitted that way from body to body, is the essence of communication.

Maybe that's why the philosophers say that I am my brother's keeper. When I am helping someone, it is really myself, but in another body or in another context. When I was experiencing the energies of my brother or my sister, I was reacquainting myself with myself. This was happening because they were in close proximity, and we were all transmitting energy back and forth via vibration. Perhaps that's an ancient form of communication, without words.

Before I was born I was learning to hear sounds and glean meaning from them. I could see my mother's feet in the sound of her running — the vibrations of her feet on the ground.

The sound my mother made when she ran was "Tolliaah-who," which in the Tiwa language I would later learn means "abundance of clarity that is aware." Even inside Mother's womb, I was already learning to think words and images before they became ideas. I was learning to think with my whole body and not just my mind. I learned how to do that before I was born because I had to rely on my mother's body to think.

We can participate in pre-birth knowing because reality is a circle. I believe that time's motion is both linear and circular. Time moves in a spiral. Traveling in time, we circle round to a place from which we can look down and see where we started. My pre-birth experiences could be known again because they existed on the circle of reality. It's just that now I was farther up the spiral.

Sound is how the physical world drinks other energies in its immediate vicinity in order to quench its thirst for existence. Sound and non-sound vibrations make up our insights — hindsights, mental telepathy, powers. All of these abilities are gifts for being alive inside our perceptions.

As a child I had a hard time knowing when I was in a visionary state and when I was in ordinary reality. Sometime after I was born to the physical world, I recalled that the birthing process was like coming out of a dark wall and spilling slowly into a dream that was made of gentle humming sounds.

After my birth, time began to carry me into awareness. The motion of time was new to me, and so was the sound that it made. It took time to tune myself to my new home of unfocused images. It was as if my life was awakening gradually to a bright light, and in it I met my parents and older sisters and brother. They seemed like giants, and in the beginning their big faces would come floating down at me from above my crib, their faces made of light splashing on me. Living in this place of light was like living in rainbows of ever-changing, colored energies. My family generated vitality in my body, and the vitality fueled my gradual awakening — my awareness of my place with them. I remember wriggling to get their attention.

I recall that as I listened to my mother and father discussing family matters over my crib, I knew solutions or possibilities for them. My conscious awareness was a glowing light superimposed over my infant body. I recall my father sitting on the bench of the army-surplus horse-drawn wagon we used for transportation and my mother lifting me up into his arms so that she could climb up into the tall, deep wagon box. From this particular day, I see pictures of sheep's heads with tags on their ears, because my mother and father were shepherds.

I don't think it was an accident that I was born half Ute and half Picuris and that my father was Picuris and my mother was Southern Ute and that I ended up at Picuris, where I grew up. I don't think we're accidentally born into families. I think we're put there for some reason and that, as we continue to live from that family and all that comes with it, we begin to grow into the reason we came here.

I think perhaps I was born to that family because that's what I chose. So I was there and now I was getting acquainted with my new relatives in a physical way, rather than in a mental way. Mind energy is cold, impersonal. Heart energy is warm. It is also ancient. That's why in ceremonies, elders say, "We invite the ancient relatives." What we are really saying is, "We bring in the heart."

Four years after my arrival, my brother Benito was born. While I was still very young, it became my job to watch over him when everybody else in the family was busy. I remember one time when Benito got hurt and I felt it was my fault.

We had no running water, so my parents hauled water from the ditch, put it in a big barrel, then built a fire around the barrel to heat it for washing. My sister Mabel used to heat water for us to take a bath every Saturday.

One day my mother and sisters were washing clothes. They had taken the tub off the fire and the fire had gone out already, so only the ashes remained — or so I thought. Apparently, however, there was an ember or two. My little brother Benito, still in diapers, crawled over to the ashes. I can still see him very clearly. He sat down, and as he sat he began to shriek because his feet were on the embers. I remember running and then my sister came and my mother came, and they lifted him, but his foot had already been burned.

I felt it was my fault my baby brother got burned because I hadn't stopped him from putting his feet in the fire pit.

Our life in La Boca seemed filled with accidents. When I was about five years old I went with my father across the river to cut hay. We were riding a horse-drawn alfalfa mower with a sickle on it that would turn and cut the hay. We had a new horse, Sandy, that my father had broken to the harness. He harnessed Sandy to a more seasoned horse and then we went into the pasture and he put me on Sandy's back, where I rode, holding the forks that go on the collar. When my father was finished mowing, he took the mower and lifted it out, then he took the horses over to the gate and dropped the reins to open the gate. As he was coming back around to get the reins, the horses took off with me still on Sandy's back.

As the horses ran, I bounced forward and back until my head hit one of the forks, crushing my skull where it entered my head. The next thing I knew I was in the hospital. Nathan Bird, a family friend who had a truck, was working as a ditch rider for the Bureau of Indian Affairs at the time, and he took me to the hospital. The doctor operated and I recovered, though I still have a hole in my skull about the size of a dime.

While the doctor was operating on my head, I found myself floating outside my body, watching him. I could see everything this young doctor was doing. I could tell he was not very sure of himself. I watched the operation from above my body, looking down, completely removed from fear and pain.

++++

I am able to see in hindsight how all the experiences that I had as a child and later as a young adult and then as a full-grown adult were directly connected to my purpose in life. I think that maybe that's the way it is with all of us. Without realizing it, we are led in a particular direction. We are not always aware of the reason, but it takes us wherever we need to go, even when we don't know that's what's happening. All we know is that in some way everything's perfect.

When I was traveling in Germany during the 1980s, angels who presented themselves as men in their late forties would appear and help me load my suitcases at train depots and train stops, then they would disappear. I believe that they were sent by the Great Mystery to guide me, to protect me at railroad stations because of the incident where my two sisters were killed. The angels told me they were there for my protection, and their presence kept me from being afraid of trains.

Years after Corleen and Gloria were killed, my brother Fernando Rael had a child, and he named her Corleen Gloria.

Perhaps the two sisters had returned through his daughter to be in the persona Corleen Gloria, and maybe my job was to raise her. I did raise her; for fourteen years she lived in my household and I raised her as my own child. Maybe that was a way of making some amends for encouraging my sisters to go down to the tracks.

Everything in nature balances out.

Everything has meaning.

A Man With Six Names

I AM A MAN WITH SIX NAMES. When I was born, I was given the name Earl Head. Earl was the name of the doctor who came to the house and delivered me. Head was my mother's last name, given to me because at the time we lived among her people, the Southern Ute.

My father was Alfred Rael of the Tiwa-speaking people of Picuris Pueblo in northern New Mexico. When we moved to Picuris, I received father's last name, Rael. In addition, the cacique, or holy man, of the Picuris Pueblo, Antonio Simbola, gave me a Tiwa name, "Tsloot koi yeh," or, in English, "Beautiful Painted Arrow."

When I was ten years old, after my mother had died and I had gone to live with a foster family at Picuris, I was baptized in the Catholic Church and given the Christian name Joseph.

Several years later, in the church in Ignacio, I also became Michael. And when my first child was born, we named him after me. I became Michael Joseph Earl Rael, Sr.

My great-grandmother was the sister of Chief Severo of the Utes, and it is out of that line that my mother comes. My mother was part French because once upon a time a Ute Indian man met a trapper who used to come down from Canada and they became friends. They agreed that if the Indian died, the Frenchman would take care of his family. So he did. The Frenchman married the Ute widow and from that union came the woman who was my great-grandmother.

When she was eighteen years old, my great-grandmother contracted smallpox and the Utes couldn't cure it because it was new to them, so they left my great-grandmother and another young woman who was sick by the side of a trail near Conejos, Colorado. They left them there where the Spanish would find them, thinking the Spanish had a cure.

When the two young women were found by the Spanish, they were taken to the Spanish governor, Sr. Cabezon, in New Mexico, and they did recover. Cabezon raised my great-grandmother and the other woman until the time of the repatriation when the governor gave my great-grandmother back to the Ute tribe. Chief Severo recognized her as his sister and remembered the stories that were told about the two girls the Utes had left behind. My mother's maiden name was Head, Beatrice Head. Head in Spanish is *cabeza*.

My father's lineage contributed the Rael name, which, I think, had something to do with my destiny as a visionary.

In the era in which Spain was sending people to settle New Spain, now north central New Mexico, there was a Spanish explorer named de Vargas in the area, and he had a lieutenant named Rael. They both had children at Picuris. From this came a family with the Vargas surname. Likewise, the lieutenant, Rael, had a son by a Pueblo woman, and the child was named Rael. He was my ancestor.

Now, here is something very important to me. The Rael name comes from the original word "Israel." The Raels were Jews who were running away from persecution in Spain. They were called *los conversos,* meaning those who converted to Catholicism in order to keep from being killed as Jews. The name Rael on the family coat of arms means "bearers of light."

Maybe in fact I was destined to play the role I am playing in the world today because it is the unfolding of that particular mystery of the "bearers of light."

II. CROSSING TO PICURIS

The River

WE LEFT LA BOCA, COLORADO, to resettle in Picuris Pueblo, New Mexico when the Second World War had come to the Pine River Valley. Manuel, my older brother, went off to the army, and my two brothers, Tayo and Fernando, and I left with our father, Alfred Rael ("Redfish") to go to Picuris, to his people. Our mother followed soon after. I was about seven years old.

Our trip to Picuris seemed very long. I slept, woke up, and slept again on my father's lap in the cab of the big truck that belonged to Nathan Bird, my father's friend. My father had commissioned him to drive us, and he had agreed. Only a mile from Picuris Pueblo, between Vadito and Picuris, we had to cross a stream, and we got stuck.

"I knew we shouldn't have come this way," said Nathan Bird with his forehead leaning against the steering wheel.

To break his sense of helplessness, my father opened the door and let us out. My brothers left, running up the hill, and

I immediately went right down to the river's edge to watch the slow-moving currents. As I stood there watching the river, suddenly, off to the left, I saw something move. I looked. Nothing. Again, to my left, something moved, and this time I saw a little person about my size, perhaps smaller, but bright with living light. He sat across the bank looking at me and asking me telepathically with his big, round eyes for an invitation to be friends. I said yes, so he ran on the surface of the water, kicking and splashing, to my side of the stream. He was a warm heart, and he stood smiling with his hands behind his back, leaning against the river bank.

I asked with my mind, "Who are you?"

He said, "I live here."

He knew our truck was mired in the river and communicated this by sending me a ray of light from inside his eyes. In the instant that he did this, he also communicated that everything would be all right. He said that his relatives would lift the truck from underneath and guide it to the other side of the creek. All of this he said in that one flash of streaming light. Instantly I believed him. Somehow, I knew that what he was telling me was true and possible. I remember he gave me all of this in visual images. I was listening with my eyes and seeing with my ears.

He asked if I wanted to play by walking on the water as he did. I said Yes and without thinking stepped out onto the surface of the stream. I instantly fell down to my waist in the water. I knew he was as surprised as I, for as I sank into the cold water watching his face, I saw my falling experience in his thoughts. I also saw in my mind's eye an adult mouth speaking with a reprimanding voice from across the way. It scolded him; perhaps it was an older brother or parent. I looked to see but did not find anyone there.

My father was calling me from the direction of the truck, so it was time for me to leave. I saw a flash of him, too, in my mind's eye. I tried telling my father about my new friend, but he did not hear me. He and Nathan were too busy preparing to drive across the stream. They were both wet to their waistlines and moody. When Nathan started the truck, it seemed to rise of its own volition and then float the rest of the way, right to the other side.

As a child growing up at Picuris, when I was finished with my duties, I would go sit by that stream to visit my river friend. He never reappeared, though I often sensed a pair of eyes watching over me.

Years later, when we were both working for maintenance at the Ouray Ute Cemetery, I asked Nathan Bird about that river crossing. He still remembered how the truck had floated across, even though, he said, "the wheels were not touching."

He said, "The thing that got me was that truck ran across like someone was pushing it, or carrying it, guiding it across the water. I never could figure that out."

I never told him about my friend. By then I was learning to keep my mouth shut.

In later years I realized that two beings well known in the

mythology of the Tiwa-speaking people, Elf Boy and Old Man Beaver, had helped us across the river that day at Picuris. For a moment inside of warped time, we were in their myth and they were in ours.

In fact, I used to see the "little people" in Colorado all the time. In the summer we would sometimes do a tree-spirit watching ceremony. We'd go up around big trees, lie down on sleeping bags, and just watch. Pretty soon, we'd see the lights of the trees, almost like they were Christmas trees, and then we'd see the beings of the trees. They would manifest into some kind of humanoid appearance or something else. That's the essence of little people.

When I saw Elf Boy by the river, he was not very big — about three feet tall — but he wasn't a troll or a dwarf. He looked more like a kid with big eyes. I think he was the spirit of the river or the spirit of the bank, the vibration of bankness. He showed up, and I thought he was real.

That experience happened near Picuris. Later I would be taught that the whole canyon where Picuris Pueblo is located is made up of sacred sites where the human anatomy is honored. If we wanted to honor one part of the body, we would go to a particular site in the canyon. We could ask for healing and offer cornmeal to that particular form, and healing would come. We could touch a particular stone and it would be the same as touching the liver, or the heart.

Elf Boy and Old Man Beaver were also spirits inhabiting that canyon. As I grew up in Picuris, I would learn about them in the Picuris children's stories. In one tale, Brother and Sister Fawn are running away from a goblin-like character. Then they get to the river and they ask Old Man Beaver to carry them over, so the beaver carries them on his back. The little people I met were the essence of that archetype.

A New Language

WHEN I ARRIVED IN PICURIS, I knew three languages, Ute, English, and Spanish. But the language people spoke most in the pueblo was Tiwa. In order to fit into this new place, I would have to learn to speak Tiwa as fast as I could. I listened very carefully to the words people were saying, to the interrelationships between the words and their meanings. Very quickly I made a discovery that helped me to learn Tiwa more easily. I found that in Tiwa, many of the words are onomatopoetic — they sound like the things they are describing. For instance, Tiwa uses three words, *taa chi who,* for "person walking." *"Taa"* is stepping forward. *"Chi"* is the sound your legs make when they pass each other and rub. *"Who"* is the second foot stepping forward.

I loved my Tiwa name, Tsloot koi yeh — "Beautiful Painted Arrow." I loved it from the beginning because in "Tsloot koi yeh" I can hear the sound of an arrow being released from the bow, flying through the air, hitting its target and, as its feathered end vibrates, painting the air around it with beautiful colors.

I would soon learn that the Tiwa language contains in its sounds the esoteric meaning behind all of material reality. Each word, each sound, is a metaphor expressing some aspect of the Great Mystery. The world-view of the Tiwa-speaking people is encoded through metaphor in their language.

I don't think I would have learned this about Tiwa had I not been a half-breed coming in from the Ute reservation and having to learn the language at age seven.

There are certain challenges that are put to half-breeds, people who are of one tribe and also of another. I think they are put there purposely by the Universal Intelligence as a way of cultivating people who will be able to take those two cultures and catapult them both to a higher level. Evolution comes from struggle, from two entities colliding. Out of that struggle comes something better.

Early in my life, I came to know myself as split. Since I was born to both the Southern Utes and the Picuris, I was neither fish nor fowl. When I was with the Utes, the Utes would say, "Well, you're not full-blood; you're half something else." Then when I went to Picuris, I found a culture that was different from the culture of the Utes, and the Picuris would say to me, "No, you're half something else. You're not whole." This created a potential for me to think the way I ended up thinking, in two different ways at the same time.

When I moved to Picuris Pueblo, where people spoke the Tiwa language, I also moved from a mentally-oriented way of perceiving reality to one based in intuition.

Whereas before I was learning how to see life through mental constructs, now the Tiwa language and culture were requiring me to think as if all things in life were sounds, energies, vibrations. My first instructions at Picuris were that all material or non-material forms are alive and, secondly, that all of life is for the sole purpose of revelation — that everything we do or see teaches us what the No-thing looks like. This is important because, essentially, we do not exist; therefore, we are born to learn the meaning of non-existence. Non-existence wants us to know Its meaning, so we come to participate in states of concreteness which are perceptual. Our life here is a dialog between abstractness and concreteness.

My life as a half-breed living among the Utes, then the Picuris, then the whites, has taught me the difference between mental perceptions and vibrational perceptions. With a mental perception, the human psyche first apprehends and then quickly assigns placement, definition. With vibrational perception, or intuition, definition is not necessary, because vibration unfolds the essence of the thing perceived. The perception comes with a resonance. It comes complete, like a flower, or a song. Instantly we perceive it in its fullness; we drink its light and it becomes a part of us.

In visions I have seen that thoughts are like packets of light energy spiraling fast, moving forward and in a circle at the same time. As a child at Picuris, I learned to think like that, linearly and circularly at the same time.

This was confusing for a while, especially when I went to school. Here I was exposed to white ways of thinking, which are linear, and in many ways the schools tried to invalidate the circular, holistic way of thought. I had a hard time abandoning one for the other because it was as if I was losing my personal integrity. I chose not to deny either aspect of myself, so I became a maverick.

It was like walking out of one room into another. When I walked into the English world, I pretended to be English. That's how I could learn. Then I had to watch, to know when to be Tiwa and when to be English.

Thus, as a child I was already being led in the direction of duality, of being a maverick, and of being different no matter where I was. This was stressful, and that stress was also part of what would make me who I am today. I think stress leads to struggle, struggle takes us to effort, and effort culminates with accomplishments that lead us forward.

When I was seven years old, after the move to Picuris, I had a dream which contained the vision for my most important work in this life, though of course I didn't recognize it at the time. Going into dreamtime, I saw an elderly woman smiling, and in front of her were seven tiny oval-shaped music houses that seemed to be singing with human voices. As she watched the singing and chanting, the elderly mother cried tears of joy.

The vision disappeared. The next day I asked the adults around the kitchen breakfast table about it, and they responded by laughing at me and joking about my weird visions; ever since my accident on the runaway horse, I had been my mother's "child with the broken head." Perhaps because of their teasing, I put the dream-vision out of my mind and didn't remember it again until almost fifty-nine years later. By that time I had seen the singing houses in other visions and had dedicated over eighty oval-shaped peace chambers all over the world, where people meet to sing and chant for world peace.

++++

My experience is emblematic of what all of humanity is experiencing at this moment in our history. As diverse cultures come together and different ways of thinking clash, there's stress, tension. Because of this there's more capacity for the visionary to come forth and take the front of the world stage.

The very tension of masses of people in turmoil creates new insights for the overall population. Out of these insights new determinations are made as to how — socially and politically — we are going to develop in the next twenty-five or thirty years on the planet.

We are all evolving into another way of thinking. Rather than flowing down like the natural current of the river, we're flowing upstream, and we can only do that on the supernatural level because on the physical level, everything is controlled by the laws of gravity and entropy. Out of the conflict of many cultures, we are evolving into a new form of human, able to do things humans have never been able to do in the past.

When I was at Picuris and beginning to learn its culture, I discovered that in order to be accepted by the other children and the elders who were teaching us I had to learn what I was being taught so well that it compensated for my being different. I learned Picuris tradition. I learned how to speak Tiwa better than the other children who were also learning the language. I learned how to do ceremony better. I wanted to be wanted. I wanted to be liked. I wanted to stop people yelling at me for making mistakes, because I was making a lot of them. I was forced to take notice of things that children don't normally pay much attention to. Now, all the people who were teaching these ceremonies are gone. As the years went by they died, and I became the only one who knows the meaning behind all the traditions.

Something happened, though, that I found enlightening. I had different teachers for different things at different times in my life; some were men and some women. My grandfather, Antonio Simbola, was my main teacher. After he and other men and women who were also my teachers died, they came back and continued teaching me. I would be doing a ceremony and I couldn't remember something. Then all of a sudden, through the side of my eye, there was a presence. I would look and see no one. Then I would have a strong sense again of someone there and I would look again and find no one.

A few times I caught sight of someone's arm long enough to recognize it, and I knew I was seeing someone who had died a few years earlier. The person would be present in the room, and I could just ask about something I needed to know, or I could use my intuition. Then I had to learn how to trust that intuition, which was another kind of challenge.

One example of what I learned at Picuris has to do with color. At ceremonial times it was the custom for the dancers to paint their bodies. By painting my body black, I became the breath of the voice, that power to speak and to hear. I called into myself, and into the ceremony for the village, the power of the void, or the No-form, to speak through into the form — in essence, the power to create. The white paint called in the power to break free of obstacles. The power of the blue paint was the power to venture into unknown territory. The yellow paint opened new doorways of opportunity.

Sometimes, when you belong to one tribe and not another, you are met with racism. I think racism comes when we first experience polarity. In consciousness, we have the male, the female, the positive, the negative. I think racism begins there. When we are born into tribes, a natural conflict arises because tribalism is a form which is very nationalistic. It preserves its own essence. It's concerned about purity. Conflict comes because we are either man or we are woman, we belong to this tribe or that, and there is tension between groups. Conflicts are natural in this earthly reality, so, apparently, we come here in order to experience conflict.

Most American Indian writers are half-breeds. Not many full-bloods write books. I think this is because half-breeds are trying to integrate the different aspects that split them down the middle.

I believe the legacy that we leave is the whole planet's multiculturalism, where a lot of different people are coming together. When Hitler came into power, the rest of the world just looked the other way and didn't do anything about the spread of fascism and racism. Now we're no longer willing to do that. We cannot afford to let racism continue, because we know better. We have come to the planet at this time to embrace our differences and heal the conflicts.

My Mother's Death

NOT LONG after we moved to Picuris Pueblo my mother died. She was having trouble walking and they said she needed a goiter operation because her neck was very swollen. She had an infection, so they took her to Santa Fe Indian Hospital.

Before she went to the hospital I had a vision in which I saw her in a coffin. Then, two days later, an ambulance from the clinic in Taos came up toward the house. It had a hard time because we were a mile off the graveled road, but it slowly made its way up our muddy lane and turned around. A nurse and my father went into the house and brought my mother out in a wheelchair. As she was getting into the ambulance, she called to me. My other brothers were at the door of the vehicle saying good-bye, but I hung back in silence. I was afraid that if I said good-bye to her she would really go, and that if she went, she would really die. I knew death was connected with her illness, because I had already seen her in the coffin. Because I thought this, I did not say good-bye to her.

From the ambulance, she said, "My son doesn't love me any more, and he won't tell me good-bye," and she left. In that moment I knew that my mother was gone forever, and I was never going to see her again in exactly the same way I had seen her. It was as if my whole world ended. The next time I saw her she was in the coffin. I never got to say good-bye to her, and I never got to tell her how much I loved her.

A very deep loneliness came into me after this, into my lungs actually. I carried loneliness for many, many years until I went to a shaman who did a ceremony with me in which I took some ayahuasca. Ayahuasca is an hallucinogenic concoction from South America, and it opened up my lungs. It was as if I had recoiled when the grief struck my heart, I had doubled over in a fetal position that compressed my lungs. The ayahuasca ceremony opened my lungs again. Afterward, I was no longer susceptible to allergies and colds.

Living with Lucia and Agapito

AFTER MY MOTHER DIED, my father was not able to take care of us, so we were sent to live in different foster homes at Picuris. I became the foster son of Lucia Sandoval Martinez and her husband, Agapito Martinez. My father placed me in the household of the Martinezes not long after their adopted son Filbert died in the Philippines in the Second World War. They didn't have a son now, so I went to live with them and be their son.

I didn't really want to be there, because I wanted to be with my biological parents. But this was not possible because my mother was gone and my father could not maintain the household. All of my other brothers went to foster homes or to boarding schools. I believe my father farmed us out because he wanted us to be constantly blessed by the powers of inspiration. That's the way it was.

Lucia and Agapito were wanting to heal the pain they had because their adopted son had died, so I filled his role for them for a while. Every now and then, Lucia would make a mistake and call me by Filbert's name, and Agapito would too. Filbert's father was Apache, so like me he had been a half-breed, part Apache, part Picuris.

Lucia belonged to the Sandoval family of Dulce, New Mexico. She was Jicarilla Apache, but she married into Picuris when she married Agapito Martinez. I was raised in that household, and I was the only son they had. I did all the farm work that was required, harnessing the horses, hitching the horses to the wagon, and working in the gardens. We planted the field in the spring and in the fall we harvested the crops. The whole village worked together, planting and harvesting, doing ceremonies. As part of that whole community, I had five or six teachers at any one time, teaching me about different things — how to hoe a garden or how to do ceremonies.

I was raised by the whole pueblo, although I was living with one family. When it came time to harvest the crops, we all joined together. It was very hard work, but we would make a big party out of it, and in the evening we would eat together. We had a center place where we brought our harvest food, and there was one house where we stored some of the grain for the next year's seeds.

Barter was a way of life at Picuris, too. One family might have three milk cows but no chickens, so they would trade milk for chickens.

I think I was born out of metaphor to participate in metaphor by participating in perceptual reality. Lucia means "light," and "the brightest star," like the morning star or the evening star. Agapito's spiritual name was Chu-quay-nay-nay, which means "Where Eagles Perch." There are four eagles, one for each of the four directions, and they're the keepers of those directions. Some people refer to them as Grandfathers. Lucia gave me the power to become enlightenment, whereas Where Eagles Perch gifted me with ability to cross beyond the doors of the four directions and disappear into their wisdoms. He never spoke of the directions to me, but he would awaken my four doorways when his physical presence was near mine.

Like the Utes, the Tiwa-speaking people had the concept of the four directions, but at Picuris it wasn't a structured teaching in any way. The concept was embedded in the Tiwa language. We were told by the Picuris elders, "Oh, you're an easterner" or "you're a southerner," or "you're a northerner" or "you're an up-above guy," or "you're a down-below guy." They never told you anything more. We danced at certain times but the elders never told us why. They did say that it kept the Master Plan going. I now believe they didn't tell us anything more because they didn't want us, or those to come after us, to get stuck in the form. Forms lead us toward attachments, and attachments glue us to a set time and place, hence suffering.

Picuris people don't call themselves Picuris. They call themselves *tuu taah teh nay* and then *pii-tah* — where the center of life is, or where the kiva is the center. "We are the people from the source — the center of the circle of light."

So, if they are the people who are at the core of existence, then they necessarily must also be the expansion of that. They're calling themselves "the No-form creating the form." This is what they represent. It's what they are. That's why they call themselves *tuu taah teh nay,* which suggests that they don't exist, but also suggests that they do exist in states of non-existence. Non-existence is what gives validity to existence. Non-existence is black, and existence is white. The first story the

Picuris storytellers tell is about Magpie Tail Boy and Yellow Corn Woman. The magpie is black and he also is white.

I didn't want to be in that foster home situation, but I was taught early on that children were to be seen and not heard, so I wasn't allowed to express my feelings. The adults would tell me what to do, where to go, to haul water, chop wood, do whatever ceremonies needed to be done. In that household, children were not allowed to speak their minds. That bothered me for the longest time, and I still don't know what that means, but that was the way Agapito and Lucia were. That's how they wanted their household to be. I needed to live according to their rules, so I learned about following rules, and that would be, in the end, the most important teaching of my life.

If you're going to be a successful human being in a spiritual priesthood, you have to learn how to listen to the inner voice of the spirit, and you have to learn how to follow orders. When something important comes to your awareness, you don't question it. You act on it. Because I wasn't allowed to question anything in that household, I learned early in life to do what I was told.

Last summer a woman came to see me whose mother was going to have surgery on her hip. I said I was willing to dedicate a dance that we'd be doing in Australia in October for her mother's healing, and, since I wouldn't be going to Australia for another three months, her healing would be retroactive. Her mother went to the doctor two days later. They didn't have to operate because, apparently, the hip was healing. Her healing took place months before the dance for her healing took place.

I said her healing would be retroactive because Spirit told me to say it, though it didn't make much sense at the time. If I get a thought about something or someone, I need to act on it. I trust that some Universal Intelligence is guiding me. It's always been like that.

Learning from Grandfather

SEVERAL YEARS after I went to live with the Martinezes, my father married Marie Simbola, and her father, Antonio Simbola, became my grandfather. He was the cacique, the spiritual leader, of Picuris Pueblo, who had given me the name Beautiful Painted Arrow. As the cacique he was the one who knew when all of the ceremonies were supposed to happen throughout each calendar year to keep life going. His job was to go out and say, "OK, it's your turn. You're the clan who's supposed to do this and that ceremony."

And we went along because he was running things. We had a limited number of people around Picuris because young men and women were gone to war. It was left up to us to carry on the traditions — children nine, ten, eleven, twelve years old. We had to learn the ceremonies from the cacique. Each clan has its role to play, and members of one clan cannot go and see what other clan people are doing. Yet, if three males were supposed to be in the ceremony and there weren't three grown males from the right clan, then somebody had to step in.

When grandfather would go to do ceremonies in the kiva that belonged to him, he would invite me to go with him. Even our approach to the kiva was part of the ceremony, walking up to it, descending the stepladder into the underground chamber.

In Tiwa thought, when you go down into the earth, you are going into the spiritual center of the Vast Self. The moment you start down the steps of the ladder into the chamber, you become the Vast Self. The Tiwa language was structured so that we would naturally think of and see everything around us in this way.

The walls were alive and the stepladder, made of wood, was alive. The stepladder was a living being that carried us down into the chamber. As soon as our feet hit the floor there was a sense that we knew who we were. We knew what life was, and therefore, we knew that we were life. In this context, the chamber is a hologram, the three-dimensional resonance of *tau-lee-uu-tah* — point of light that acknowledges abundance. Light is thought, and abundance is expansion of pure clarity. *Tau-lee-uu-tah* — point of light that acknowledges abundance — was the name of the chamber. When we came into it we became its purpose for existence.

All the kivas, including Grandfather's, used to burn sage in the chambers, and this would purify as well as heat the space. We would wait until most of the smoke had dissipated before entering. When we first came in, it wasn't smoky enough that we couldn't be there, but it was smoky enough that when we left the chamber we smelled like sage.

Burn: *loin* — to cast life down toward the inner self where all knowing lives

Sage: *taah-uu-lo* — to clear a pathway to divine self

Heat up: *leh-lee-aah* — to bring up ancient wisdom into conscious knowing

Smoke: *kuuh* — to open receptivity

Once Grandfather began singing in the kiva, his songs seemed to take us into a place of transcendence where it was very easy to see visions. Often we saw sacred dances, almost like movies projected on the wall, but they weren't really on the wall so much as they were just a foot or two inside the wall. We could see images of people walking, sometimes men, sometimes women, sometimes children.

Each thing we did and each thing that existed in the kiva was a metaphor for some spiritual form. Sitting was *laa-aah-ii-eh:* bringing clarity to awareness. Singing was *chaa-tah-hu:* creating the presence of Source. Wall was *naah-pooh:* wiping clean the screen so that wisdom could be projected for the person watching.

Many times all we saw were colored lights — red, green, blue. In some of the ceremonies Grandfather would ask in prayer for these lights to slow down because they were moving very fast across the screen. They would slow down, stop, and then would pulsate just in one spot. If they were doing that, he was receiving information, which he was responding to. It was all happening in a language we didn't understand. (At least I didn't understand the language.) But we knew for certain it wasn't Tiwa. Grandfather would communicate maybe with the blue light, or maybe with the red one, for ten or fifteen minutes, and then it would be gone.

I could hear the lights talking but I never knew what was being said. I think the lights were holograms — energy forms — stalking him and teaching him principles of the World of the Dead. What he told all of us was that there were many realities in existence and the colored lights were one of them. He explained that they were principal ideas. These ideas were manifesting in this reality, maybe in the principle of running or standing or walking, for instance. He taught that once he acquired knowledge or wisdom everyone in perceptual reality got it as well.

Grandfather was actually trying to teach us about image and sound — how images have sounds and sounds have images. Over the years I noticed that he wasn't praying for anything particular. I was there with him from about 1941 until the mid-forties, about four or five years. But my training actually lasted longer, till about 1948, because after his death he kept coming to teach me in dreams or visions.

One day there were four of us children, two girls and two boys, in the kiva with him. He lay with his body facing the fire and asked us, one at a time, to lie behind him with our backs to his back. He said that we would see lots of little lights going on in our heads, so to keep our eyes closed. Today I believe this was a transmission. He was transmitting information from his back through our backs into our bodies.

When I was about eight years old, Grandfather told me to go into his kiva for a special ceremony done only once every hundred years. He sent me in there to do this ceremony by myself. I asked him what exactly I needed to do. He said, "Just go in there. You'll know when you get there."

I went into the kiva alone and I was alone in there for many days. A little old lady we called Wee-oh-ney, who lived across ther river, came into the kiva at the same time twice a day to bring food and to carry out the chamber pot and empty it.

The food she brought was a special diet, mostly made of corn. There was no fruit, nothing like that, and little salt. She brought cornbread, sometimes corn on the cob, sometimes corn stew. If the stews contained any meat, it was a small amount of venison (*peeh-waa-ii-eh-ney*: to see how life is continually placing itself in total awareness). Most of the stew was corn. Corn is *ii-hooh,* which means "to allow what is known to die so that new potential can emerge."

There's a kind of corn rust, a black fungus that grows on the corn. That was central to the soup. Years later, when the white extension agent used to come around, he would find one of those ears of corn with the rust and he would say, "This is bad." He would throw it out. Of course, the Indians would come in behind him and pick it up and take it home because it was very nutritious, apparently. The black fungus was what I was being given to eat in the kiva. I think it helped me to expand my perception of what was happening both in the kiva and also later in my life.

Every once in a while, beings would come into the kiva. Spirit beings would come out of the wall and sit, and there were lights. There were vibrations that fed me. They actually fed me physically, and I felt full as if I were sitting at a table eating food. I also felt full emotionally and mentally as if I were being loved. I felt emotionally fulfilled as well as mentally stimulated.

To this day I don't really know what this ceremony was about. Grandfather didn't explain it to me, or why they did it every hundred years. I don't think he needed to, because I have it in me. I think that I was the ceremony. My presence was central to it because I'm a two-legged, and the two-legged has a different kind of resonance than a four-legged. So, I think what he was trying to achieve was the resonance of the two-legged. By the resonating power of two-leggedness, I think I was part of a discourse with all the other powers of the four directions that make up the center of knowledge, the center of wisdom, the center of the circle.

Sitting at the center of this ceremonial chamber, which is

round, I became the connection with the center of the circle of light. The light and sound beings were aspects of the circle of light, and I was the center of that circle. Of course, now I know it as the medicine wheel. I saw the medicine wheel through the lights that were emanating from it. Circle means to go forth and sow seeds, to plant them as lights that life can drink to sustain the soul of its being. I saw the lights of that center and I heard choruses of many voices singing in harmony. It was beautiful music of a kind I haven't heard in this reality, but the closest to it is the human voice. The sounds would be oscillating in the room with the colors. Sometimes they would fly all over the room, like rainbows, like fireworks on the fourth of July, fast, but non-threatening. The music was such that I was in a state of awe continually.

These lights and these energies were feeding me physically so I wasn't ever hungry. I was on a high — a physical, mental, emotional and spiritual high — for long periods of time, but at the end of it, there was no exhaustion. I never felt I had extended myself too far physically or emotionally, but rather, when it was over and these lights were gone, I fell asleep. I would just continue on a slower resonating vibration into deep sleep. The kiva was a very gentle, peaceful place where I could rest without fear and wake up the next morning energized. I didn't really want to go anywhere else. I didn't feel a need to go outside or to find something to entertain myself. It was good just sitting there and being quiet. I was free of my normal boyhood need to run here, run there, run free.

Finally Grandfather came in and got me. "You've been here for so many weeks. You know, you were supposed to come out."

I said, "What do you mean?"

"Well, you were supposed to come out after so many days, but you stayed a little longer than we thought you would. But, because you stayed longer, we decided to leave you in here because maybe we needed to do something different in your case."

++++

At Picuris Pueblo, all of the children — boys and girls alike — were taught as if they were someday going to be shamans or sun priests or heads of different clans. Then, after a certain training period, they would go to their separate clans for more training.

I belong to the Clan of the Thunder-callers, so I was trained specifically for that area, although I had other training as well. As a Thunder-caller it would be my particular responsibility to do ceremonies to call the rain to come water the crops. Grandfather trained me.

Agapito used to take me into the mountains as a youngster. He would ask me to shout and then listen to the echo of my shout. His instructions were basically that our echoes feed our souls. In the same way, what we see, we swallow in order to sustain us morally and keep us physically alive.

Picuris world view does not have a hell or heaven. We are

morally good because we are continually drinking physical sunlight and non-physical, spiritual light. Since we do not exist, we stay alive by seeing with our physical eyes and then by our insights. I have a brother whose name is Tayo, whose spiritual name is Mountain Echo, Pii-tooh-chell-low. The tradition at Picuris is that when my brother dies and crosses over, almost immediately after his death, a new member of the tribe will be given his name so that the resonance of Mountain Echo will continue among the people.

In Tiwa, "sound" is *naah-pooh*. *Naah-pooh* literally means "I am hearing myself."

Most of what I do today as a shamanic healer came from visionary experiences I have had in ceremony, while fasting — taking no food, no water — and dancing. Some, however, I learned growing up at Picuris. The power of healing that came to me during that time has shaped my life. I learned to trust the healing power and to discern what practices were to be kept and used in healing. My awareness of this started when I was about twelve years old. I began to figure out why certain experiences, certain potentialities, were coming into my life. I found I could use some of my visions in healing ceremonies. The ceremonies that came first in vision were always successful.

As a member of the Thunder-callers Clan, I took part in kiva ceremonies with other young people for extended periods of time. It used to take us six weeks to bring the rains in the spring. The Spanish-speaking people surrounding our Indian village would ask us to come call in the rain, and Grandfather Simbola would lead us on a run — fifteen miles down from the top of the mountain — as part of the rain ceremony. In spring we brought the rain, and in autumn we brought it again for moisture to help the fruit to ripen.

During one autumn ceremony when I was about thirteen, I was in the kiva with two young men, sixteen or seventeen years old, and other boys my own age.

We were getting ready to go and bring the thunder. As part of the ceremony we had to go up into the mountain and then run back down. There were some plum trees near the ceremonial chamber, and one of those days just before we went up to bring in the thunder, one of the older boys said, "Well, I know the elder said we're not supposed to eat this, but look at these plums. They look so good."

I looked at one and I just couldn't resist, so I took a bite and I liked it really well. I said, "I'll eat just a little bit of it. I won't eat a lot of it." So, I just ate part of one plum, not quite half of it — a small wild red plum with a bitter skin. Then, we did our run up the mountain and back down to the kiva. When we got back, the next part of the ceremony was to blow through a reed into a bowl of liquid. Usually, when we blew through the reed, lots of foam would come out of the bowl. I started blowing into the reed and into the bowl, but nothing happened. No foam. Of course, the elder looked over and he said, "I bet you ate a plum. You been eating plums?"

At this point I decided I might as well tell the truth. I

always had difficulty not telling the truth anyway. So I told him, "Yes, I have eaten a plum."

He said, "Well, we're just going to have to wait around here another week or two."

So, we waited another two weeks and then we went up the mountain. We walked up about fifteen miles. At the top, the elder covered us from head to toe with mud and got us ready. Just as the sun was coming up, we started running down the mountain. He stayed right behind us yelling, "Ah mah pia! Ah mah pia!" which means, "Hurry! Hurry up! Run faster!"

After maybe six or seven miles, I was starting to feel exhausted because we were going up and down rocky trails. Then at some point there was a shift and I had the sense of something like wings above my head. I didn't see any wings, just the other boy who was in front of me, running. Behind us, Grandfather kept shouting, urging us to go even faster. He knew it was necessary for us to run to the very limit of our capacity to achieve a certain level in the ceremony. At that level power would enter, a power that was required to bring a blessing to the village.

Of course, the blessing is not just for the village; it's for the whole world. Ceremonies at Picuris were never done for just one individual or tribe. Each ceremony was done for the whole world, for everyone, the dancers included.

Now I was not sure whether I was still running or whether I was the eagle flying. As we descended the mountain and ran into the village, I remember the villagers shouting, urging us on. They were overjoyed to see us come down the trail. We ran all the way around the village and then over to the place where the race ended. Here two stones stuck up from the ground and we were to feed them with cornmeal. I remember reaching into a pouch on my side and taking out some cornmeal even before I got to the stones.

When I got to them, I fed the shrine by sprinkling the cornmeal on the rocks, and as I did, I fell backward suddenly, as if thrown to the ground. The people were yelling and shouting because we had put in the effort that was required. As we runners lay on the ground, exhausted, the people of the village started "feeding" or blessing our bodies by sprinkling us with cornmeal. I was in another dimension.

And as they fed our bodies in the same way we had fed the stones, we could feel thunder rolling in. Then finally it was really present, and we could see it — lights like static electricity crackling and sparkling about eight feet above our heads. An electrical mist hung over us like a cloud, and a yellow light was present inside it. I don't know how long we were there, maybe half an hour. Then, just as it came, the sparkling mist suddenly went away. The thunder had come for as long as it needed to, and then it left. It never stayed longer than it was supposed to; that is to say, it left after the prayers were finished. We could see it crackling as it receded above us and then it was gone. I came into ordinary reality.

We all got up and went down to the river to bathe. Most of the clay was gone, but now the mud was mixed with perspiration. After I washed my body in the river, I put back on the moccasins I'd worn to run all the way down the mountain.

Prior to the run, the elder had fixed our moccasins, taking the thicker part of a deer hide to reinforce the soles. All our clothes were made of deer hide for this ceremony, because, he said, "Don't mix metaphors. If you have a shirt made out of deerskin, don't put on buffalo hide shoes. You have to put on all buffalo or all deer." For this particular ceremony, deer was required. Deer energy brings focus to existence. Buffalo would be used for the planting vibration. We call the buffalo "kaah-ney-ney." *Kaah* means to plant.

One of the most important Picuris ceremonies happens every August on Picuris Day. The men go up on the mountain and cut a tree from which they make a tall pole to plant in the center of the pueblo. Most pueblos, including Picuris, have sacred sites extending for many miles, maybe over a hundred miles, in all directions from the center of the village. The pole will be set up at that heart, that sacred center place. As part of the day's ceremonies, there are races between the men and boys of the summer people and the men and boys of the winter people. They run not so much to compete as to bring blessings to themselves, their clans, the entire pueblo, and the entire earth. There are also dances near the pole. These dances have to be done carefully because each pattern of steps is sacred — every single step is sacred.

At some point in these ancient sacred dances, clowns come in and start mimicking the dancers and messing up the steps. They make fun of the dancers and spectators. The clowns shake everything up. They come in and do this as a way of saying, "Stop taking yourselves so seriously. Don't get stuck in the form." I think the clowns are the most sacred aspect of the whole dance.

I have come to believe this is my main role on the earth. I'm the clown coming into the dance to shake things up.

Beginnings as a Medicine Person

AT TWELVE I started doing healing ceremonies, and people got better. I didn't know why, and I didn't want to know why. Whenever it was important to do a healing for someone, the situation always unfolded to make it possible for me to do it. I was getting put in certain places at certain times so that certain experiences could come to me.

The first healing ceremony took place while I was at the house of my grandfather. A man and a woman came in a horse-drawn wagon to get a healing from him. They stopped in front of the house, brought some groceries in, introduced themselves, and said they were from one of the pueblo villages. My grandfather agreed to do a ceremony the next day for the lady who needed a healing. That night we just ate dinner and went to bed.

The next day we had breakfast together with the man and woman, and then we sat down. Grandfather called me over to the side and said, "You had a dream last night, didn't you, Beautiful Painted Arrow?"

"Yes, I had a dream last night." I was surprised that he knew about my dream.

Then he said, "Your dream has to do with the healing we have to do for this lady, so what did you dream, because your dream will tell me what needs to happen."

So, I told him the dream. Grandfather sat there for a while, and then he said, "You know, she really came to get a healing from you."

"Yeah, but I'm not a healer. I'm just your grandson."

"Well, but the dream clearly says that she came to you for a healing. This is what we'll do. She thinks she's coming to a healing with me. It's OK. We'll just let her continue to think that, but you remember that part of the dream where you have to use water?"

"Yeah."

"At some point when I'm doing the healing for her, I want you to come in. You'll bring some water in as if you're bringing it to me, and I'll ask you to apply it as if you're doing it under my supervision."

The woman's problem had something to do with her back. She had been having difficulty for years, and now she was almost paralyzed. I could see the blood flowing and I could see where it wasn't flowing, where it was getting plugged in her veins, so I applied the water, just plain water. I can still see my hands, a child's hands, very small, putting water on her back.

At that moment I really didn't want to be there, because I was afraid. I don't know if I was afraid of my power or if I was afraid of making a mistake. I wasn't very comfortable, but I put the water right down her spinal cord to the tailbone. I applied it about four times from the base of her neck all the way down her spine and then over to the place on her back that I had seen in the dream, where I saw there was an affliction. She started trembling and jerking up and down. Grandfather was holding her down, and I was standing there afraid and not knowing what was going on. I thought maybe she was dying or maybe I did something wrong. He said, "You just wait there." She was having trouble breathing or something, then she stilled.

All of a sudden I saw light coming from her as if she was translucent. Right after she stopped shaking, she was in some kind of shock. She went from a purple light to an almost translucent state, and I saw it happen right in front of me. She opened her eyes and I could see they were full of amazement and surprise but, at the same time, of joy. She got up and she was well, healed on the spot.

Later I asked my grandfather, "What happened? How come she got well like that? Is that the way they get well?"

He said, "No, they don't always get well like that. You have some power that you were born with. That's why you can do that."

"Well, what caused it?"

"I think it was the dream."

That's all he told me, that it was the dream and we had made the right interpretation of the dream.

Later on, when I was eighteen years old, when this same woman was dying, she came back to Picuris. She came to Grandfather's village to die even though she was from San Juan Pueblo, because he had been her healer. The people had a big feast for her at Picuris. The elders did a ceremony for three days because they said the particular illness that she was carrying was for some reality on the other side of the cosmos. They did that ceremony for her because she was connected to those people on the other side.

Some of the illnesses we carry here, we are carrying as a gift for folks on the other side of the cosmos. Grandfather's idea of healing is that illnesses never happen just because they happen. It's not just because we don't take care of our bodies or we don't eat properly. He thought it was connected to some larger purpose or condition. He believed that people die when they're supposed to die.

He said, actually, we never really die. We drop these bodies, but we never die.

I kept doing healings after that. People came, and I just knew what to do, what they needed. I worked with Grandfather until he died.

I was about fourteen years old when he died. Before he died, I remember hurting my knee; he rubbed it with ashes and it just healed itself. I had taken it out of the socket, and he put it back and then put some ashes on it. After this I walked like nothing had ever happened. Amazing healing powers came through him.

I sometimes have that same ability. Even today, it comes and goes, and I don't know why. Sometimes the healing power is present and sometimes it's not present, but I always know when I'm in that state. It can go for two or three months, or two or three days. Then I might go into the dark night of the soul and I go for six months with nothing. I sense that I don't have the capacity or something is missing in my being that is not allowing this power to come through for healing.

After a while, I began to realize that everything I did throughout a given day or week or month, including healings, was in rhythm with a larger resonating vibration. Whatever part we play is whatever part we play, but it is in line with, and in tune with, the larger whole. I'm not talking about just the earth, but other realities, other parallel realities. We all belong to a big chorus, and we're singing our part.

Any healings that I did when I wasn't with Grandfather, I'd do without letting people know I was doing them. Once I left Picuris and went to the Indian School, and later in high school, I concentrated on my schoolwork, not on doing healings. But I did them now and then. For instance, one time a person was having difficulties — she used to smoke a lot — and there was some talk that they were going to have to take her to the hospital. They found out she had lung cancer. When

I heard this news, I sat down in my bed in the boys' dormitory at the Santa Fe Indian school and I concentrated. I just asked that she be healed. Some time during the night that particular affliction or lump or whatever it was, fell out into the lung cavity. When they went to operate, the spot was starting to close where the tumor had fallen out, so they sucked it out, and she got well.

Another time after I became an adult, while I was living in Bernalillo, New Mexico, a woman next door to me had lung cancer. They rushed her to the hospital, but I did a healing for her at my house and she got well. I have done many, many more healings at a distance than I have face to face.

I was in Tulsa, Oklahoma, once doing a workshop for the Indian center, when a young Indian man came up to me and said, "My friend is in the hospital. They're going to operate on him." The doctors had done a biopsy and they knew he had cancer. Because he was very obese they were afraid he would not survive the surgery. The young man asked me, "Could you do something for him?"

He asked me this as he was driving me to a sweat lodge ceremony. We did the sweat lodge, and when the ceremony was over I had some tobacco left in a little bag that I had taken out of the sweat lodge. We were going to eat, and the people were going to do some drumming, and then I was going to leave. I had driven from Albuquerque to Tulsa to do the ceremony and give a talk, and then I was driving back. The young man asked me again, "Could you give me a ceremony for my friend?"

"Yes," I said. "You know that tray they roll around in the hospital?" I saw it in my mind's eye. "Well, there's one near his bed. Spread this tobacco out on it, then get some water and put it in a glass till it's about three quarters full, then put the tobacco in it and let it sit for three or four minutes to get energized. Then tell him to take it in three separate swallows, and he'll be all right." This was a ceremony that I saw in my head. Before he left, he asked me again, and I knew by then he was having some doubt. I remember very clearly telling him, "Look, you don't have to believe it, I don't have to believe it, no one has to believe it. Just do the ceremony." So, he went, and he and his friend did the ceremony. On Wednesday of the following week, the friend was scheduled for surgery, but the doctors examined him first and found the cancer was gone. Instead of going into the operating room, he checked out for home.

After I left, people in Tulsa tried to give me credit for this, but I said No, that all of us healed him. I've never tried to take credit because I don't think it's me. I think it's the Spirit. If I'm gifted to experience healings with people, I am grateful. Whenever somebody asks me for a healing, I consider it an honor. This is my opportunity to serve. I try not to get involved at the ego level because that shuts off the energy.

Beyond the ego level, on the pure spiritual level is real joy. That's where I try to live.

III. SCHOOL

Day School

I HAD TROUBLE WITH MY EYES as a child and I didn't know what was wrong. I needed eyeglasses, but I didn't get them until I was twelve. This made things difficult, especially once I entered the Picuris Day School. Here, in a one-room schoolhouse, I was taught reading, writing, and arithmetic in English, by a white teacher, beginning when I was seven.

I sat in the back of the room and relied on the boy next to me to help me read the blackboard. One day when I was in about third grade, the boy who sat next to me didn't come to school, and I couldn't see the lettering on the board. I was frustrated. Then, I began to feel a tickling in my ears, like somebody was tickling me inside my head and I heard a voice say quite clearly, "Why don't you ask the blackboard to come to you?" So I said, "Blackboard, come to me." And it did. It moved forward, I read it, and then it went back.

I also learned in the third or fourth grade at Picuris

Pueblo Day School that I could sometimes know all about a book and what was in it simply by slapping the book. I don't know how I figured out I could do that. I just thought it one day, and it worked. I think there was some Universal Intelligence around me that was telling me that. So, I slapped a book I was supposed to read and a light came from the book and engulfed me. Immediately I knew what was in that book and all about the author. I got quick flashes of visual images, moving really fast, of a man sitting at a table writing the book — an older man.

This ability would be a great help to me in college and graduate school. I could walk into the classroom and talk about the book as if I had read every single page and maybe even studied that writer for years. The information I got that way was perfectly clear and right.

All my life, stuff like that has happened. Half of me feels as if I just live from the time I get up until the time I go to bed at night. I make appointments with people, and I do the normal things that I need to do. But I know that now and then incidents are going to occur that are supernatural. I look forward to those moments, and I'm always in a state of expectation.

Some days in grade school I would skip class and just go up in the mountains by myself. Here I had a different kind of education, with the earth and the plants as my teachers. Running in the deep canyons of the Picuris Mountains and on the ridges, from the corner of my eyes I used to catch movement — movement of the plants wanting to play. They would appear and then disappear quickly. Knowing that they were hoping to be noticed, I would try my deer eyes and capture them in my vision. When I use deer eyes, I open my eyes as wide as I can, stretching them and keeping them wide without blinking as long as I can. I would hold the plants in my deer eyes until we could talk telepathically.

Cheh means "eyes" in Tiwa, and *kwe-el* means "that which is locked in place." *Puuh* means "to be cast away." Apparently our eyes are locked to the daily perceptual reality we live in; therefore, we program our eyesight not to see too many of the vibrations in our lives. That is because we do not want to be distracted by unwanted trivia. Once I apply "puuh" (to-be-cast-awayness) I can then see with deer eyes, not only the image of the physical plant, but additionally the spirit that usually steps outside and stands beside its plant home and talks telepathically.

The plants taught me to eat them for their medicinal properties because they enjoyed traveling the human digestive tract, through the pleasing landscapes that could only be found in the human anatomy. I would eat the leaf of a plant, and then I would wait fifteen counts. The plant part I had eaten would send back a report to the plant that had given the leaf and translate the messages of the eaten plant leaf back to me. The transmission had to be done quickly because after fifteen to twenty seconds the eaten leaf of the plant went into a pure bliss state and connections were lost.

"Body" is *tu-nay* in Tiwa, and *tu-nay* also means "to crystallize the power of carrying the experiences of the Vast Self in a pure clarity of awareness." I used to do this with the plants while I was skipping classes from the Picuris Day School, and in this way I learned that we are all the Vast Self playing here in these individual bodies, drinking this world's light.

Santa Fe Indian School

I WENT TO THE SCHOOL at Picuris through grade school, and then in seventh grade left home to attend the Santa Fe Indian School. This was a boarding school where boys and girls from a number of different tribes in the area came to live, study, and learn the ways of white society.

The school had a strict regimen. For instance we quickly learned to fix our beds in a proper way. I enjoyed doing something well, so whatever I did, such as making the bed, I always ended up doing according to the way they wanted it done. The floors were linoleum and we were taught to keep them well swept. They were waxed regularly, and on Saturdays we would get the polisher, a big machine, and we'd polish the place. Once we had it all dusted and polished, Mrs. Haskie would come in and inspect our work. There was a ledge, and she would run her hands over it. If she found dust, she'd say, "You're going to get a D here."

We got very good at finding dust and making sure that we passed inspection.

I had never used a flush toilet until I went to the boarding school in Santa Fe, and I was fascinated by the sound of the gushing water. Flushing toilets quickly became my favorite pastime until I got caught by the boys' advisor.

There were two or three boys to a room. Sometimes we'd have jackknives and we'd turn a wooden chair on its back so the bottom underneath the seat would make this nice little target we could throw knives at. That worked for a while, but the knives kept chipping wood off the bottom of the chair until pretty soon we had a big deep oval where the wood had been, leaving just a very thin seat. None of us wanted to sit on that chair because if it broke, the person who broke it would really be in trouble. Invariably, somebody would come along who didn't know about the chair and would sit on it and fall to the floor. Then we would end up having to pay for it and we'd get put on the fatigue list. Fatigue list meant extra duty — kitchen patrol duty.

The usual reason I got on fatigue list was because I loved to sleep. A bell would ring at six-thirty in the morning to wake us up for breakfast at seven o'clock. Classes started at eight o'clock. Sundays we were expected to dress up in slacks, a dress shirt and usually a jacket and tie.

I didn't have any dressy clothes, so when I first arrived at school, I used to borrow clothes, such as a white shirt, from the other guys from Picuris — in particular from Bernard Duran. He would supply me with shirts, mostly because he didn't want to see one of his countrymen looking like he needed some help. All my clothes were hand-me-downs from cousins, relatives from Picuris, so they were very well worn.

As a twelve-year-old boy, I hated having to wear worn-out, borrowed clothes all the time. Finally I decided to enter the chapel at the school campus and pray about this situation. I asked in the Tiwa way for financial assistance. Four days later the advisor at the boys' dormitory came to ask me if Earl Head Rael and Joseph Earl Rael were one and the same person, because he had received a check for $400 from the Southern Ute Tribe in Colorado via the BIA, IIM account in Ignacio, Colorado. Then I knew that Tiwa prayers worked as well in the chapel at the Indian School as they did in the kiva at Picuris.

When I went to the Indian school in Santa Fe, I had pigeon-toed shoes that were starting to fall apart so I tied them with copper wire to keep them together. I loved those shoes because they were really comfortable, but they didn't look very handsome. So, it wasn't very long before I had to go shopping for some new shoes. I found some, and in order to pay for them, I went to work for one of the motels across the street from the Indian school there on Cerillos Road in Santa Fe. They had garages that used to collect dust. For sweeping out eight garages, the motel manager would give me fifty cents. I would do that over the weekend, and after four weekends I had two dollars. You could get a good pair of shoes for six bucks back in the forties, so I worked three months, then went downtown and bought the shoes. After that I kept working so I could have money for other things, like movies. Back then, you could go to a movie for forty-five cents.

At age twelve, thirteen, fourteen, part of our education required that we learn etiquette. To teach us manners the school would provide a banquet and we would be encouraged to ask someone for a date.

For the occasion, we would have to dress up in a coat and tie. We usually didn't know the girls very well and most of us were shy. We didn't know how to behave, so they would teach us. "You can't use this fork for that." They'd have classes in home economics. We had to take "home ec" just like we had to take general shop and carpentry. Then they would teach us how to set a table, how to eat, how to be polite and how to swallow, how to drink water, how to hold a glass. They taught us how we were supposed to treat a girl when we sat down to the table.

I was constantly embarrassed because I could never get it straight. After we got home at night, the instructor would gather all the boys and we'd talk about our mistakes. I don't know what they told the girls, but I was glad I wasn't there to hear what they said to them. We were a bunch of Indian kids; we didn't grow up in that kind of society. As a matter of fact, some of the time I was growing up, we didn't even have a table. We ate on the floor.

Before my mother came to live at Picuris, we lived with my grandmother who cooked all of our food in micaceous clay pots in the fireplace. She boiled everything, then she would spread the live embers in the fireplace and lay the meat right on top of them. We didn't have a stove, so everything was done with fire. We didn't have any coal. We used firewood.

But the dirt floor was swept clean and we had cloth mats. My grandmother would buy twenty-five- and fifty-pound bags of flour and use the bags the flour came in as cloth for napkins and place mats for the floor. Eating was a ceremony. We would use little dippers made from gourds. She would do some singing about the bowl, about the food. The significance of eating was a major Picuris teaching. We were taught that everything was eating — that life was eating all that lives, and all that lives was eating life — that the soul was drinking light. Life was providing the food for us and we were life's food.

This was how we ate in the home of my grandmother when I first went to Picuris, sitting cross-legged on the earthen floor. It was a ceremony, so it was done very politely. You weren't allowed to slouch. You had to be very straight, to be respectful. I liked it because each meal was something special, and we were doing it three times a day. While we were sitting on the floor eating there was no room for anything else except piety, being connected through reverence.

Grandmother died and with her went an era. Later, in the other Picuris households, people had tables. People began to say, "Well, we don't adhere to so much of that old stuff. We want to move to the way we were taught at Santa Fe Indian School." Lucia and Agapito had also been to boarding school. They still wanted to maintain the old forms, but now they were doing it on a table rather than on the floor.

Things were changing. We were moving from the old ways to the modern ones over three or four generations. That's what I saw. It wasn't until much later that I realized every object on the table was a holy thing and the table itself was holy and eating was holy and the three meals that were served were holy ceremonies. Within the words the people were using — every word they used for every object — within the word itself was the power of that essence. From early childhood we were being taught to be caretakers of all that is holy. That role makes life joyous.

At my grandmother's I started to see that the power of language was right within the words themselves. When we did ceremony, we could bring those powers into existence by verbalizing them.

At the Santa Fe Indian School we were required to go to church before we went to Sunday dinner. Those who were baptized Catholic went to the Catholic church. Those who were Baptist or belonged to another church, were picked up for services elsewhere. Sometimes they would send us to different churches to see if we liked them because some students weren't sure whether they wanted to be Catholics or Baptists. The school was trying to make us into Americans so that we could get along. Wherever we went we could get along with the Lutherans or we could get along with the Methodists, and all of those churches wanted us.

The Santa Fe Indian School was run by the Bureau of Indian Affairs, which operated Indian boarding schools throughout the country, and that's where the Indian kids went.

We were taught English, history, and math. They also had vocational training in those schools so we went to carpentry for six weeks, to bakery for six weeks, then we went to art for six weeks, and so forth. By the ninth grade we were required to decide which vocation we wanted to go into, like silversmithing, maybe, or farming, or general shop. Then, that's where we went for tenth, eleventh and twelfth grades.

I studied art for six semesters over a period of three years, in seventh, eighth, and ninth grades. I also chose farming, so I had chickens. I got them as little chicks and raised them as part of my project because I was learning how to be a farmer. I had about thirty chickens at the end of the term. Then I realized that maybe I wasn't cut out to be a farmer, so my father ended up with all the hens. He picked me up at school in his truck and we loaded all the chickens and took them back to my foster parents' place in Picuris, where we had to make a big coop for the roosters. We had fine roosters for cooking and the whole village ate well as long as they lasted. Of course, my dad had a lot of surplus eggs so he supplied us with eggs. He lived away from the village proper where he had a small ranch, and that's where he took all the laying hens. My foster parents ended up with all the roosters. Later I decided that my dad got the better deal.

But art was what I loved to do. In seventh, eighth, and ninth grades, I studied art with some well-known Indian artists, including Velino Herrera, who was married to my stepmother's sister from Picuris, and Gerald Nailor, a Navajo who was also married to a woman from Picuris. I used to sit and watch Gerald Nailor draw and study what he did. Flat art was popular in the 1940s, and it is still what I do today.

The students at the Santa Fe Indian School included mostly Pueblo Indians and a few Navajos. Some members from the Ute tribe also came down to school.

We were all just trying to learn the American culture and do whatever our teachers expected of us. I noticed certain characteristics of the different tribes. The Hopis seemed to be a lot more intelligent than some of the others. They were fast learners. I think the other group that was very intelligent were the Picuris. The trouble with Picuris students was that we lacked preparation when we got to Santa Fe. At the Picuris school we would get a teacher for two months and then she'd quit. Then we'd get another teacher for two months and he would quit, so there were four grades reading the same pages in the one-room schoolhouse.

When I went to the Santa Fe Indian School in the seventh grade, I didn't know my multiplication tables, so I had to sit in the front of the class, which was embarrassing enough, and be drilled using flash cards. There we all sat, all the Picuris kids, learning to multiply. By the eighth grade we were caught up with the rest of the class. By the ninth grade I was doing work at junior-college level, not just in reading and writing, but also in math.

The home room teacher for seventh and eighth grades, Mrs. Killerlain, helped me learn my multiplication tables and took time to show me how to study. I used to go and wash windows for her on Saturdays to earn a couple of dollars for a new tie or a new pair of trousers. I think now that I was trying to discover the windows to my life. What can I see from this experience? What did it all mean? Out of somewhere would come an essence, an understanding.

We were required to learn to dance. I hated social dancing at first because I was all feet and all thumbs. But it was fun once I got the hang of it. Mrs. Zamero taught us how to waltz. She would draw a big square on the gymnasium floor with tape and say, "You start over here. You put your left foot over there and your right foot over there." Then she would turn the music up really loud in the gym and we'd be dancing there by ourselves, all the boys on one side and the girls on the other side. Then she would say, "Go pick a partner." The girls would be sitting there, then she would say to the boys, "You gotta use your etiquette."

Here we were, a bunch of twelve- and thirteen-year-olds from the pueblos. I remember one boy so awkward nobody wanted to dance with him. He asked a girl to dance and she refused. He must have kept insisting, because pretty soon she just got up and cold-cocked him. Down he went. I said to myself, That wasn't very ladylike! My mother had said that girls were angels.

Once we learned to dance in class, we had parties where we were required to practice our waltzes and two-steps and dress properly in a suit coat and tie.

Later, when I came out of school and was working, I wore a three-piece suit. I knew the etiquette. When I went into business for myself in the 1980s, I met people high up in government and in different countries. I sometimes hung out with wealthy, sophisticated people. I felt confident doing this because I knew something about etiquette.

In home ec we learned about cooking. I had already learned a little bit from Lucia and Agapito, but in home ec they taught us how to read a recipe, how to put ingredients together, and how to set the table. Then we went to art, and they taught us how to mix paints to obtain certain colors, how to use a brush, how to sketch things out first on a pad and then how to take that sketch and make a painting. Our teachers did not give us books to read about drawing. They showed us how to do it right on the blackboard, and we were required to copy. Then at some point, they said, "OK, now let the energy of the universe come in through your hands and through your mind and draw whatever you want." So, that's how my art started.

Some of our teachers were Indians and some weren't. The art teachers were Indians, our coach was an Indian, and the coach's assistant was an Indian. The head of our dormitory, Mr. Shinos, had a master's degree in music; he taught the choir.

I sang first tenor in the boy's choir in the seventh, eighth, and ninth grades. In ninth grade I also went to mixed choir where we sang with the girls, an eighty-six-voice chorus. I loved the boys' choir because we learned to harmonize and sang on the radio. We also sang at the state penitentiary, and even traveled to Shalako in Oklahoma and sang there and at some of the other schools like Bacone College. With the girls' choir, we sang over the radio and for groups in Santa Fe and Albuquerque. That's where I got my background in music.

Peñasco High

AFTER THE TENTH GRADE, I stopped going to the Santa Fe Indian School. It was 1952 and the government said that Indians now could go to public schools. They started sending federal money, "Johnson-O'Malley monies," to public schools to educate Indian children instead of to the Santa Fe Indian School. The Picuris kids were sent to Peñasco High School, about six miles from Picuris. I lived at home with my foster parents and went to Peñasco in eleventh and twelfth grades.

At Peñasco, there were mostly Hispanic kids — very bright people. They were curious about me. They knew I spoke Spanish so they just figured that all Indians spoke Spanish (although, of course, they didn't). One time when a bunch of us were at the movie theater off campus, I heard one Hispanic boy saying to the others, "Don't talk Spanish around these guys because they talk better Spanish than we do."

The Peñasco High School girls wanted to check out the Indian boys. We were new and different. Some of these girls had rich fathers and fancy cars. At Picuris we didn't have anything because we didn't have that kind of culture. But girls whose fathers were working for the school or at Los Alamos had money, so they would come in their fathers' cars and pick us up at Picuris. They would come down the road and park in the village, and we would hop on their running boards and go with them to Peñasco to drink soda pop or something. That didn't go too well with the Hispanic boys who found out, so we cut that out pretty soon. I think parents got a little upset too. They said it was not good to try to mix apples and oranges.

At Peñasco I won prizes in music playing the trombone, and I also played Spanish songs on the accordion. Later I played trombone in a dance band in which a band instructor played trumpet, one of the Peñasco teachers played saxophone, and a classmate of mine played the drums. One time when we were playing for a Peñasco school dance, I got to do a solo, the trombone part of "Stardust."

Standing there in my striped trousers, I was really scared that I might make a mistake. When the band instructor looked down at my legs and started laughing, I looked down to see what he was laughing at and almost started laughing too, because my trousers were shaking. I managed to finish "Stardust" without breaking up, but I never forgot that image.

In the twelfth grade, maybe just because of luck, I became president of the student body for Peñasco High School. One of our tasks was to develop by-laws for the student council, studying the by-laws for some of the other schools in the area. That was the beginning of my interest in government. Also, I used to go with my father to various tribal gatherings in which Picuris met with other tribes in New Mexico.

My school experiences took me into the white, Western world with its scientific mode of perception. Now and then, however, a mystical experience something like those of my early childhood would break into my everyday world.

When I was seventeen, but looked old enough to pass for twenty-one, I would sometimes go out bar-hopping with my friends. One night in a bar in Gallup, I met a fellow on his way to California who had stopped for a beer, and we ended up making a night of it. Early the next morning we hired a room near the railroad tracks. When we woke up, we started out to get some breakfast. Suddenly we saw an old Navajo man flying over the railroad tracks like Superman, but wearing regular clothes instead of a cape.

The guy I was with said, "You know, I really have to stop drinking. I think I'm going home." Then he just turned around and left.

College and Marriage

I GRADUATED from Peñasco High School in 1954 and from there went to Colorado, to the Southern Ute Reservation. I was married in 1955 to Patricia Lucero, a Southern Ute woman, and we started having children. Our first child died at three months. Her name was Joleen, and she died a crib death. That was deeply shocking. I was still in my teens when it happened. Soon after, we moved to Albuquerque where I enrolled in St. Joseph College but didn't finish the first semester. I just dropped out.

Patricia and I had five children. Two were born in the same year, eleven months apart. We were married for eighteen years, from 1955 to 1974. After we divorced, I provided child support for the children until they were all grown.

In March, 1958, when I was twenty-two, I was injured in an explosion in Bayfield, Colorado, where a house I was working on blew up. In the explosion, my rational mind expanded to include a vision that would carry me for the rest of my life. Ten of us were in the house putting in pipes, when somehow gas ignited. I must have been thrown out of the house by the explosion. The next thing I knew, I was lying on the ground away from the main blaze, and there were fires everywhere.

As I lay on the ground, unable to hear because of the deafening impact, I saw an image of the Virgin Mary standing in front of me. She said to me, "You will be all right." Then she disappeared.

After a while my good friend Sylviano Valdez, whose house we'd been working on, carried me to another house nearby. I ended up with two broken legs and a fractured back. I remember being taken to the hospital in a basket rather than on a stretcher.

Why did the Madonna appear? I think when my body was broken up, my life force asked for some sign that I was going to be all right, because I thought I was going to die. The Madonna is visualized as the Mother, and the Mother is a metaphor for expanding that-which-is to something larger. When I learned that the universe began with a big bang, I began to understand the relationship among creation, expansion, and sound — between vibrations and states of living essence.

The human psyche tends to want to expand, not simply because of greed, but because it's in the natural order of psyche to expand. When it expands, and then contracts, it achieves a new state of being through that cycle of expansion and contraction. The psyche then has a new flooring on which to stand. It has a new self-empowerment that it can fall back on in order to continue a higher, more balanced dedication to life. I believe that was what was happening when the United States went into its period of westward expansion in the 1800s. Expansion and contraction can also be achieved inwardly.

In 1968 I entered the University of New Mexico at Albuquerque. I was thirty-three. I went to college because I wanted to know what was in those books and what it was to go to college. I wanted to meet other people and talk with them and get some experience. It took six years to get my BA. I was working part-time and raising five children. I got help with tuition from government and state loans, and the tribe gave me $1,200 a year for books and other expenses.

It seems to me that all of my life there has been an uncanny presence taking care of me and my human affairs. I must say, though, that I have not had much luck with long-lasting relationships. Relationships with women never seemed to work out well, and heartbreak has been a constant companion. Maybe that was one of the reasons the spirits took care of me, because I never knew when to get out of the way.

I was still working on my BA at UNM when Patricia left for Ignacio, Colorado, with the children, and I ended up with a trailer house in Bernalillo (where I would later have the vision to build sound chambers and where I would build the first one). I continued working and sending support payments monthly. I then married a lady named Ruth, and we were together for five years. My third marriage lasted roughly five or six years. I never married again after that.

In 1974, I decided to learn more about politics, so I went to the University of New Mexico's political science department and asked the department chairman if I could take a master's there in political science. He said he would check into it. "By the way," he told me, "there is a girl from one of the pueblos who is having difficulty in political science and you have a background in the subject. Maybe you could help her." Of course I didn't, and that was a mistake. When I asked him if I could come into the master's program a couple of months later, he said, "Well you know, I asked you to help this woman and I guess you didn't, so you'll just have to go somewhere else." Then I realized again that you have to do what you're told.

I was engaged to Ruth by this time. She was from Lake City, Minnesota, about two hundred miles from the University of Wisconsin in Madison. On a trip north I visited the University of Wisconsin's political science department. The chairman looked at my grades and said, "You're not going to make it with these grades here in Wisconsin. However, if you can get on the Dean's List and have some extra A's, we might consider it with at least a 3.0 average." So, I went back to UNM, where I was still a junior, and got on the Dean's List. After I graduated, I returned to Wisconsin and showed the department chairman my grades. He said, "Well, you're in." Ruth and I got married and moved to Madison.

The nice thing about Wisconsin was that you weren't allowed to fail. They sent you to writing classes, or if you needed other kinds of tutoring, they would take you to tutoring. I finally asked my department chairman, "Why do you do that?" because I thought maybe they were just doing it for Native Americans or minorities. He said, "No, we do this for everyone, because we want people to be successful here and to finish their coursework. We don't want to send people out who are half prepared, because if our students are successful out there, it's good advertisement for us and that means that more students will want to come to the University of Wisconsin-Madison." That made total sense to me. I had developed an ability to read people's minds, so I knew he wasn't lying.

I had discovered I could read peoples' minds while I was still at the University of New Mexico.

I used to spend a lot of time there poking around in archives looking for information. A lot of theses written years before had never been published, and they were good. I was always poking around in the archives for ideas because I was interested in learning. I also spent a lot of time on the reservation working with some of the tribes, helping them read the federal guidelines for community action programs. I belonged to a technical assistance team funded through the University of New Mexico to provide that kind of service.

Because I was busy with other things I would come home and not always read my assignments. Now and then I could slap the book and I would know what was in it. That seemed to work some of the time, but not all of the time.

One morning I was not prepared for my nine o'clock political science class. The sun was shining that morning, and I think that had something to do with what happened, because I've always had a strong relationship with bright light. As soon as I sat down in Professor Lopshaw's political science class I started hearing a roaring sound in my head. The first thing that occurred to me was that maybe I had wax in my ear. Then I thought maybe I had high blood pressure.

I always used to sit in the back of the room because if you sit in the front, there's a chance the instructor will ask you questions and you will make an ass of yourself if you don't know the right answers. I was sitting in the back hearing this roaring noise, and I was watching Professor Lopshaw writing something on the board at the front of the room. All of a sudden, very clearly, I began to hear a voice inside my head saying what was being written on the board. I could only hear that voice and none of the other sounds around me. Apparently the spirits who were helping me had directed my attention to the board. So, I was looking and then I realized that I was reading Professor Lopshaw's mind. That was my first experience with mind reading.

After that, whenever I heard the roaring noise, I knew the voices that I heard were the thoughts of another person, or something Spirit wanted me to know.

The last time that happened in the university setting was in Wisconsin about two years later when I was taking oral examinations for my master's degree. Six or seven professors were throwing questions at me rapid-fire. I was answering them, but part of me was getting agitated because the questions were coming so fast. I wasn't being given time to think. Suddenly the roar began to build inside my head. It grew until I couldn't hear my professors' voices any more, but I could lip read what they were asking so I could still answer their questions.

At some point the department chairman started formulating a question in his mind, but he hadn't asked it yet. Nevertheless, I distinctly heard his voice asking a question. I proceeded to answer it, and he jumped off the chair about six inches. I thought, Oh, boy! I'm in trouble now, as I realized I had answered a question that hadn't been asked yet.

Later, the professors called me to them and said, "We'll

help you get a Ph.D. here at the University of Wisconsin. We'll even get you a job at Harvard — if you'll just tell us how you read our minds." I had thought people got higher degrees and jobs based on hard work and how smart they were. I said, "No, I'm going home, because I think that's where the answers are."

I had passed my orals and gotten my degree. Before I left the University of Wisconsin, I gave the department chairman an Indian drum as a going-away present.

++++

By this time, I had already decided that I was going back to my father's plan, my father's model, my mother's model. That was the tribal model, that if you wanted to learn the real meaning and power of life, you had to go back to the prehistoric forms of ceremony. All of the answers in life were embodied in the land, and they were in the people, and they were in those places I had come from.

I had come to high school and then to university from a people who said that you could get all of your information by sitting in front of a fire. Eventually the fire, when it chooses to, will teach you everything that you want to know.

As a teenager, when I told elders from Picuris and the other pueblos I was in high school, they said, "You don't have to go to high school. You can learn by sitting in front of the fire." When I went to college, they said the same thing. Now I thought, Well, maybe they're right. I'd better go find out.

Later, I would enroll in a doctoral program at the University of New Mexico because I wanted to study the Picuris children's stories recorded in 1926 by J.P. Harrington. I transcribed them with the linguistics department at UNM for Picuris.

The informant who had told those stories to the white writer was Rosando Vargas. Vargas had been banished from Picuris by the elders because he told those stories outside the pueblo and the traditional storytelling setting, and he allowed them to be recorded. I met Vargas in the 1950s when he was an old man and had been gone from the tribe for a long time. Rosando Vargas saved the stories but died in exile of a broken heart.

He saved the stories because people had stopped telling them in the pueblo. Instead of listening to stories, children were watching television. Today they've started telling the stories again in the schools, but these are taken from Vargas's books. Without the books, I believe these powerful stories would have been lost completely to the Picuris people as well as to the rest of the world.

I didn't finish my Ph.D. work. I left to find my spiritual calling in a different kind of Ph.D., a study of the doctrines that lie within the land and the sky.

IV. WORKING

Making Peace

THROUGHOUT THE YEARS I was getting my education, I worked to help my people through various government and tribal programs. I set up alcoholism counseling programs and worked for the All-Indian Pueblo Council, trying to get services to the pueblos. I did that in both New Mexico and in Colorado. In fact, I helped set up the first Office of Indian Affairs in Colorado back in the late sixties.

In 1976, I moved back to New Mexico and began work for the Taos County Mental Health Council. There I saw the need for a halfway house for recovering addicts and alcoholics. We wanted to combine traditional Tiwa spiritual medicine with western medicine to help our people, and we needed federal funds for a facility in which to do this, which we called the Tu Tah Center. But Picuris alone was not large enough to meet federal guidelines, so we would have to combine with Taos Pueblo. Both pueblos needed to sign a joint resolution asking for federal funds for the Tu Tah Center.

The only trouble was, Taos and Picuris had been in a state of war with each other for seven hundred years.

When you want to change something in Picuris, you don't go right to the council. You go first to some of the elders to find out what you need to know. So I went to Picuris elders, and they told me, "Well, we aren't going to sign any resolutions with Taos because we don't get along with them." They didn't say they were in a state of war, only that they didn't "get along" with them.

I remembered that some of those same elders had been present in about 1950 when the cacique and others emptied out the scalp house at Picuris and buried all the scalps and weapons in the ground. A few miles away in Los Alamos the first atomic bombs had been constructed and when the Picuris spiritual leaders heard about this and about the tremendously destructive power of the bomb, they were frightened. Warfare had always been part of Tiwa culture but now they decided it had become too dangerous. Mankind's weapons had the power to destroy the earth. The elders performed a ceremony to help bring peace to the whole world. It was much like the Bible prophecy of beating swords into plowshares. They gathered the village and we watched as, with great prayers and speeches, they took all the trophies and instruments of a thousand years of Picuris warfare and buried them in the ground, sending the spirits and energies of war back to the No-form.

I had been at that ceremony as a fifteen-year-old boy, and I knew when the elders said "we don't get along with them" instead of "we are at war," they were remembering this ceremony. But Picuris had never signed a peace treaty with Taos.

So, I took a chance. I went to Taos, to the Taos Tribal Council, and said, "Picuris now wants to work with Taos." Some of those Taos people who were in their eighties and nineties started to cry. They said, "We have been waiting for this to happen because we don't want to be in a state of war."

"I'm glad this is happening now before I die," one of the Taos elders said.

Now I was in trouble. I had to get Picuris to sign a peace treaty with Taos or I was a liar. As soon as I left that council, I went to Picuris and I talked to my contemporaries there in the pueblo. I said, "I want you guys to help me set up a council meeting because Taos Pueblo Indians are now ready to sign a peace treaty. I guess we're going to be ready too, aren't we?" And it worked. The Taos Pueblo Indians came to Picuris and, after seven hundred years of being enemies, they signed a peace treaty together.

Work, Effort, Sacrifice, and Inspiration

FROM the Taos County Mental Health Council I went to the Office of Indian Affairs, a state agency in Santa Fe, to work as a tribal liaison under Joe Herrera. By this time, some of the Indians I had met when we were students at Santa Fe Indian School were governors, tribal councilmen, or pueblo leaders, and so we had a rapport. I think it pays to meet people in school because later on you can communicate with them and get good things done for your people. We participated in writing up the documents that went into the 1978 Religious Freedom Act that was published in the *Register* in Washington, D.C. One effect of that law was to give Indians the right to do sun dances and other dances that had not been allowed since the 1890s.

I had studied political science because I wanted to know about government, but also because the language of politics used words that were big and complicated, and I liked the challenge of that. If there were three ways to do something, I always picked the hardest because there was something about effort that I found fulfilling.

Then, later, I found out why effort was important. Effort puts us in touch with the supernatural.

I understand now why the week before Easter in central New Mexico the Penitentes carry heavy wooden crosses and flagellate their bodies to draw blood. The Catholic Church tried to stop that practice in the forties and fifties even though, originally, it had come with Catholics from the old country, from Spain. They had brought these practices to north central New Mexico as a way of worshipping the Great Spirit.

As a matter of fact we used to commemorate Holy Week by walking from Picuris and Peñasco and Chamisal and Truchas down to Chimayo. It's about nineteen miles from Picuris to Chimayo, walking. Of course when I moved from

Picuris to Bernalillo, New Mexico, then I had to walk sixty-five miles, which is more effort, more miles to travel, to get to Chimayo. Effort is sacred because it is sacrifice, and sacrifice is what gets me to the vibration of inspiration.

Technology removes us from effort. We ride in cars and no longer walk. Walking is essential for the health of the planet. Effort means using our muscles. The body releases physical, mental, emotional, and spiritual energy which the plants and animals eat. When we remove ourselves from effort with technology, we need more and more people to make up for the loss of energy. That may be why we have population explosions. Replacing physical activity with technology makes us more irritable. Then there is no way we can expend the sugar or salt or caffeine that we consume and all this creates an air of irritability over the planet. We are prone to more conflict.

Anything we don't use, we lose. When we don't use effort, we lose the power that comes as a result of effort. Effort brings us joy and happiness. The less effort we put in, the less joy we get in return. That's a natural law. It's part of the perceptual reality in which we live.

Effort can be mental or emotional as well as physical. Sitting at a computer writing is effort, mental effort. But as we use machines to do so much of the physical labor for us, as a planet we're not applying as much effort to the vibration of Being. And without the effort the planet sickens.

This knowledge is being held by the Native American people. It is time now for them to share it. The books I have written, like *Being and Vibration,* I undertook thinking there might be people out there with similar experiences who would also share them with the general public. Then I could read their books and learn about their experiences, and I could expand my knowledge about the spiritual work and the supernatural presence on this continent.

People today really want to know more about what life is, other than just the social, economic, and political systems that we have on the earth. They are also interested in the supernatural forces that are working right along with us. We need to cultivate those forces in order to release the full potential within our social systems.

Bringing in Traditional Medicine

BY 1974 OR 1975, I already had the mindset that whenever something appeared in my life, there was a reason.

One day at the Office of Indian Affairs, people from the state corrections institution in Santa Fe came to talk to us about Indian inmates who were asking for the sacred pipe and sweat lodge ceremonies. I spoke with an organization in Gallup that put me in touch with medicine people who were willing to come to the penitentiary and bring the ceremonies to the inmates.

The Indian prisoners told the medicine people that a riot

was going to occur. Though we tried to tell the people in charge that something was going to happen, they didn't believe us. The Indian inmates were afraid, but the medicine people told them they would be protected if they would make tobacco bundles and tie them in their cells. They did, and when the riot broke out none of the thirty or so Indian inmates was hurt, although some prisoners were killed.

In the late 1970s I was thinking about developing a holistic health approach based on traditional medicine practices, because I thought this was the best way to help Indian people. At that time there wasn't much government money for Indian health care. I thought that what we really needed in Indian country was prevention. Since we couldn't get enough money, either state or federal funds, for Indian health care, why not develop a program that taught people about eating well, resting well, and avoiding addictions to smoking, alcohol, and sugar. We would take a holistic approach to health.

I tried to start such a program at Picuris, with the idea that it would be a pilot program. By this time I had moved from the Office of Indian Affairs to the Indian Health Service. Now I was working inside the hospital at Santa Fe as the alcoholism coordinator under a psychologist named Pat Brown. Through her I met Jim Halsey and Minisa Crumbo and got to know the famous singing group Jim promoted, the Oak Ridge Boys. Minisa, Jim, and their children are still my special friends. When I first met them, they weren't married, but he was promoting her art, along with that of her father, the Indian artist Woody Crumbo. Jim and Minisa have both participated in my dances.

I had met William Lee Golden of the Oak Ridge Boys earlier when the group did a benefit concert for the Taos County Mental Health Council. They presented a concert at Carnegie Hall to benefit the Tu Tah Center, the Picuris Holistic Health Center that we were beginning to try to establish in 1981 and 1982.

We began by getting the records from the Indian Health Service of all of the people at Picuris Pueblo, and we started taking blood tests and blood pressure readings and looking at the case histories of every single family unit, looking for things like diabetes, obesity, and alcoholism. We were searching for ways that medicine people could come in and start working with people.

But it was difficult. President Ronald Reagan's administration cut the federal programs under which we had been operating. And there were many problems within the tribe. By the 1980s, the Picuris people were living a different lifestyle than the one I'd known as a child. It's hard to talk to people about prevention when you have to compete with McDonald's french fries. Alcoholism had become almost epidemic, and it was very hard to talk to people about that because alcoholism is generational. Somebody was an alcoholic maybe five generations ago, and the disease was passed on from parent to child, until, after a while, it had become a way of life at the village level at Picuris.

The Vision of the Map

AROUND THIS TIME I had a vision of a map.

The map appeared in front of the wall of my office in Santa Fe, and on it I was shown perhaps ten or fifteen different scenarios playing out simultaneously. I absorbed the meaning of all of them in depth through one flash of light, replete with information. The map was radiating its own beingness from the problems in this Indian and non-Indian world.

Each scene on the map was also the representation of an idea, and all those ideas were flowing into me as I looked at the map. In a sense, I became the map, the ideas. The scenarios were awakening in me images of what I was going to do for the next five or ten years.

But I received so many scenarios for my life from the map in that single instant that now I had a new problem. I needed to isolate them and figure out what was supposed to happen next. The best way I knew to do this was through walking or through dancing.

So I began to walk. I walked from Albuquerque all the way to northern New Mexico, which is about eighty miles. I walked but I didn't get any images; I just got really tired. Only after the long walk was finished and I went on about my business, over a period of the next nine months, was I given the insights I'd been seeking, in the form of images.

What I recommend for people who truly seek insights is to take a walk. Just walk with strong intent for twenty miles, then go home and rest. Then watch. The great insights will start coming; it has something to do with walking.

Dancing does the same thing. Here's how I think it works: No-thing creates seeking. That is to say — as necessity is the mother of invention, as thirst creates the motivation to drink, No-thing is the motivating force behind seeking to know. When the mind is learning, it is drinking light energy from which comes vision.

As a child I would go out into the field with my father to plow. My father would say, "Get hold of the *taa,* like this, and put the reins around your shoulders." So I realized that in Tiwa we call the plow "taa."

When he would see a man or a woman or a child walking across the road, he would say, "*Peh wehn taa chi who.*" There was the word "taa" again. *Taa chi who* means "person walking." Now why is it that "plow" has the same name, if not that a person, when walking, is plowing just like I was plowing with the team of horses, plowing the ground and turning the soil over, preparing it for seed to be planted.

By walking you're plowing your field, making your own inner soil ready for new seeds to be planted.

I also started sun dancing. From sun dancing came the vision for the peace chambers, and other visions as well. When I had a vision, that vision always gave me directives. "So, here you are now, this is what you have to do next."

In my visions, I was directed to take my knowing, my medicine, to the outer world, beyond the Indians. I was told,

"Don't talk to Indians any more. You've done that since you were eighteen years old. Now you're forty-five. The non-Indian people need this information because they're the ones who are going to save the Indians. Until they know what's going on, not only with the Indians, but also with themselves, the non-Indian population won't be able to help themselves or the Indians. Until then the Indians are going to be doing things by themselves and the non-Indians are going to be doing things by themselves, not realizing that the cumulative energy of everything they're both doing is affecting all of us globally." I knew we couldn't work that way any longer.

As soon as I get a vision, even today, I know if it's a directive asking me to do something. When that happens, I just do it. If I don't do it, I lose the power of insight. I go into a dark state of the soul where I feel totally alone. A certain morbidity comes into my life, and I'm not happy with myself. I get stuck.

The first time this happened to me was when I was a child, after my mother died. I made a deal with Spirit: Please get me out of this depression, and I'll try to serve. *Naa-aah-uu-kwill* means to sink down into depression and then to rebound and find meaning in your life on the upswing. It was an agreement I made with myself. *Naa-yo-taah-wee-aah* means "I am my own creation." My creator self tells my action self to act.

It seems as if the Universe always gives me something right around the time that it knows I'm ready to go to the next level. I don't necessarily have to like it, I just need to do it. Then comes the next thing I need to do when it's time for that thing to happen. That's how I work my life. It drives people crazy.

My daughter Geraldine asked me one time, "Well, Dad what are you going to do tomorrow?" I said, "My plan is to have a sweat lodge tomorrow afternoon, and you're welcome to come and you can bring your friends. I'll start the fire at one o'clock because we're going to sweat at three and that will give the rocks two hours to heat. That's my plan."

Then the winds came up and the rocks were ready by two o'clock so we moved the sweat lodge ceremony to two. Geraldine said, "You know, Dad, I thought you said three o'clock. Mark went to town. I think he's going to be back but not until three, so you're throwing us off again. You shouldn't have told us anything about it, but now we're planning on it, so you just have to wait, Dad. You're going to have to use more wood." I'm very conservative when it comes to wood. So, guess what? Mark showed up five minutes later and we went into the sweat.

My daughter asked, "Did you know that was going to happen, Dad?"

I said, "No."

We got out of the sweat in half an hour, and we had just dressed when another event took place that we didn't expect. We would not have been ready for it if we had been in the sweat lodge at three o'clock.

That's the way I live. I never know how the things I do are going to turn out. I just show up and do what I'm told.

This energy follows me around, but I always know if I don't do what I'm told I will be unhappy. I used to tell my students, be sure that you follow your guidance because that guidance is in your higher interest. From that, other experiences will come to you that will enhance your growth.

Becoming a Being of Holism

SHORTLY AFTER I had the vision of the map on the wall, while I was still trying to figure it out, I had an experience with ghosts at Picuris, where we were continuing to try to build the Holistic Health Center.

We wanted to build the center from adobe like the houses of Picuris are built, and we had gotten the University of New Mexico Architecture Department involved in creating designs and drawing up plans. Then we brought Vista volunteers out to Picuris to do adobe construction.

One weekend Vista workers came to the pueblo for an adobe-making workshop. There were instructions and demonstrations, then everybody set to work. A young female Vista worker began to place her first adobe on the line of the wall. She had not put mud on the wall before setting the dry adobe brick in place, and suddenly I heard two young Hispanic males making fun of her and laughing.

Hispanics in north central New Mexico, especially around the Picuris area, grew up making adobes, and I was peeved that they were making fun of this young person, maybe twenty-one or twenty-two, a volunteer. She was innocent, beautiful, alive, and earnest, but also dumbfounded because she didn't know about adobe. Another woman was telling her, "No, you're supposed to do it this way," but the other woman didn't know what she was doing, either.

I was kneeling and cutting an adobe brick in half, chopping a straight line across its middle with a hand trowel, and when I heard the voices, I looked up to see who was poking fun at the young woman. As I lifted my head and looked around, I noticed that my brain was vibrating at a higher frequency than normal, that it felt ticklish.

Then I saw the two young men who were making fun of the girl. They kept fading in and out of my vision, so I realized they must be ghosts. I closed my eyes and asked inwardly, "Who are these two souls?" and I heard one of the voices saying, "At last, someone has seen us." I realized they were spirits trapped in ordinary reality.

Locked in this dimension, they probably didn't know they were dead, or if they did, they didn't know how to get out of here. I kneeled back down to try to reconnect with them. The only thing I got was the image of a car turning over about three miles from where we were, where the road curved toward Peñasco. Two Hispanic boys were in it, and it was a blue car.

So, I put down my trowel and stood up. I got in my car,

leaving all the people gathered around learning to make mud bricks, and I took off. I drove over to the houses around that curve and asked the people who lived there, "Did two boys die here around 1945, 1950?" I wasn't so sure about the date.

They said, "Yeah, there were two young boys. They were driving too fast and they turned over and they got killed."

What I saw and what I understood was that the boys' spirits were confused. They didn't know where they were. Part of them wanted to be here; part of them didn't know where to go, so they just hung out.

I went home and did what I always do. I took a match and said to them, "When this match is lit the curtain will open and the energy will come and take you." I lit the match, and when I did, I could almost hear the wind, as they went through into the spirit world.

The Picuris children's stories taught me about light, and I understand now why in the Catholic church at Picuris they used to light candles when somebody died. *Pee-aah* is light in Tiwa. *Pee* means "root." When you light a match or create a light, you go back to your roots. You return to the place from whence you came. These two young men went back to their roots as soon as I lit the light.

I believe the boys were made to appear to me so that I could do something about them. I didn't have any better sense than to light a match and think I could participate. Whenever something like this happens, it's because I have to do something about it. My life's map is a map of service.

++++

I didn't stay at Picuris to work on the health center after this. I left to sun dance at Ignacio, Colorado, with the Southern Utes. Many different scenarios had the possibility of playing out in my life. Maybe if I sun danced, I thought, I would be able to understand them in a more detailed way.

I left it up to the villagers to continue and to finish the Picuris Holistic Health Center. Well, now, twenty years later, they have a building there, and they call it the Holistic Health Center. Hopefully, later they'll have a dietitian, a clinician, and other important resources. But it's moving; it's happening.

Recently I met with a medical doctor in Tucson who is participating in the sun/moon dances I started. She practices medicine and also works with holistic ideas. I went to see the clinic she is setting up. It costs $500 a day to get in, and they do everything I would have loved to do in the holistic health setting at Picuris Pueblo.

I think that what I was doing at Picuris was planting a seed for the future of medicine. In 1980 not many people were interested in holistic anything.

Without realizing it, I had become the very being of holism. You can't work with the knees and not work with the other parts of the body as well because the whole body is going to be affected by the problem with the knee. If you have an ankle problem, the rest of the body is affected. So, that's what I was learning through my vision of the map. Although I had understood this intellectually, I didn't comprehend how it applied to the health problems of the Indians until I had the vision.

The map was part of the vision. Another part showed the reservations depicted as islands of poverty, impoverished because they had starving souls. The Indians were dying for lack of spiritual nurturing. They had plenty of food to eat, but they were dying because they no longer had the buffalo, they no longer had the game to hunt, they no longer had the things that once sustained their culture. But there were some things that the Indians had that they needed to share with the non-Indians. Indians didn't want to share with the non-Indians because of their history. The Indians were saying, "You took our land, you took everything from us, now what you want to take is our religion." The map directed me from the Age of Reason to the Age of the Heart. It was now time for the Indians to show the non-Indians how to think through the heart and not through the mind.

So, I started sharing the teachings that I had received, and over the years I have been all over the world leading workshops and ceremonies. I did not teach any specifics of the Picuris ceremonies. What I got at Picuris was a foundation.

The children's stories I heard so often at Picuris Pueblo taught me how to think — to live as if I were perpetually in a state of omnipresence. I didn't have to translate this knowledge into supernatural power. It translated itself and became part of my repertoire, based on the vibration of the land.

I have learned over the years that I should always follow whatever happens from the place of the unexpected. From the place of the unexpected, Spirit talks to me. I cannot ignore the thing that comes through from left field. When it happens, I know it's right on, even though logically it shouldn't be happening. Sometimes I want to ignore it because my plan does not include this unexpected thing.

All of a sudden something happens and I'm going off in an unexpected direction, but I know there's a reason for it. I know there's blessing there. The blessing will unfold as the week goes by, or within the next month, because that's the way it always is with the unexpected.

V. SEEKING

A Shift in Direction

DURING THE YEARS I WORKED in Indian health and social services, I didn't actively seek visionary experiences. I would go to ceremonies at Picuris or on the Southern Ute Reservation when I could, but I was holding an eight-to-five job to keep body and soul together. Eventually I left all that to seek Spirit. I wanted to spend more time doing spiritual work, and I figured that being an independent consultant would allow me to do that. I could work for three months, then stop and do ceremony for four or five months, then work again. I began to realize that it was more important for me personally to stay in touch with the spiritual than it was to stay in a traditional job.

Thus in 1980 I began freelance consulting. That's how, eventually, I came to make peace chambers and do ceremonies all over the world.

Leaving took some courage, because I didn't know if I could make a living; my contract with the government paid

$20,000 to $24,000 a year. But more and more people were coming to me for guidance and help, and programs needed consultants with my background, so I took the leap and began doing freelance consultant work for the tribes as well as the government. I was hoping my income would go up. Instead, it dropped by more than two-thirds the first year. But it started to pick up the second year, and eventually it surpassed my contract salary.

Alternate Realities

ABOUT THE TIME I went freelance, I was asked by Joe Quanchello, the governor of Picuris, to train the runners who were going to commemorate the three hundredth anniversary of the Pueblo Revolt of 1680, when the Pueblo Indians drove the Spanish out of New Mexico. The race was going to occur on August 6, so at the beginning of August I did a run with the Picuris racers, just a practice run from Picuris over to Ojo Caliente.

Before the practice run, I went by myself to look for an old trail I had heard existed in that general vicinity, an ancient trail from Picuris to Ojo Caliente. Accidentally, I went too far north, to the place where Picuris says you shouldn't go because it is where landscapes are always changing. "Aah suh naa," they call it. *Aah* means "lights," *suh* means "where the light is always changing." *Aah suh naa* means that you could walk in this place and all of a sudden be in an alternate reality. But at the time it never occurred to me that I was in the land of Aah suh naa.

I was looking for the old trail, so I followed one of the ridges where I thought the trail was, and as I traveled I realized that I was in a very strange place. The landscape started changing. I was down in a very deep canyon with heavy growth, when I noticed that the fish in a nearby stream looked strange, with enormous heads and small bodies. All I could think was malnutrition.

Then as I traveled further down, I came to a waterfall that plunged two hundred feet to where the terrain leveled out. To get out of there I would either have to walk four or five hours along the side of the canyon, or I could find a way to scale down the cliff with the waterfall toward level terrain.

As I looked down at this waterfall, I heard a voice behind me say, "Take the pole and scale the side of the cliff." I turned around and there was a ten-foot pole, so I grabbed it. Remember, I was taught by Lucia and Agapito to always do what you're told. I didn't question it. I just took the pole and started to scale the cliff. The only thing that crossed my mind was that I'd never seen a mountain climber use a stick to scale a mountain.

At first I used the pole to steady myself, and then I noticed that a force was coming periodically to push the pole against the cliff. The ten-foot pole would clamp onto the side of the rock as if it were held by a magnet. Then I would move over a bit and it would loosen. That's the way it went all the way around the waterfall. I would put my feet on ledges to keep from falling. Where the water hit it was slippery, but some force seemed to be holding me there.

When I got to the other end, there was a beach with mounds of sand. I almost sank down to my knees in that sand. A hundred feet further down were some cliffs.

I started to run as fast as I could away from these mounds of sand. But I had started a landslide. With rocks pelting me and sand shifting under my feet, I ran until I came to the edge of a cliff and there was no place else I could go. I grabbed a piñon tree, but its roots started to come loose from the soil. I then spotted a spruce tree and, taking a deep breath, jumped for it. I caught the very tip and held on as dust and rocks rained down around me. When it cleared a little, I scaled down to the bottom of the ravine on that tree.

As a little child, I had heard the Picuris legend of Magpie Tail Boy. In the story, Magpie Tail Boy is stuck on a cliff. Elf Boy comes by and tells him to jump onto the spruce tree and scale down the tree to the bottom. As I was scaling down the tree, I wondered, did I become the story of Magpie Tail Boy, or did it become me?

When I walked down and looked back through a gap in the mountain, I could still see the waterfall. Then I walked along the river until I came to the road. My wife was waiting for me there, so I got in the car, and we drove back to Santa Fe.

I have returned four or five times since, looking for that place, and I have never been able to locate it. I found places that looked similar to it but I've never found that waterfall.

The Tiwa Stories, Language, and Perceptual Reality

IN PICURIS I heard the stories about Magpie Tail Boy every year, starting when I was eight years old. That first year in Picuris, the storyteller came and told the story, then he came again the next year and told that story again. He told it the third year and the fourth, and pretty soon I was twelve years old, then sixteen, then eighteen. I was still hearing the same stories, told in the same words in the Tiwa language, but something very interesting was going on. At some point I began to realize that these weren't just stories; they were constant powers in my universe that were unfolding as daily scenarios in the village, or wherever I went.

Then, every once in a while, I'd be walking down the street and all of a sudden find myself in a whole different town or in a whole different reality. I was still sane and I was still totally in control of my faculties, but I was walking in some other place. Then it disappeared, and I was back where I had originally been. This started happening so regularly that, after a while, I didn't think much of it. I just thought, "So what? That's the way life is."

The Tiwa children's stories added to the repertoire of what was to become my perceptual reality and helped me to jump from one world to the other. I was probably already nuts when I was born, and I know I was telepathic before I was at Picuris, but these stories seemed to enhance my paranormal powers. If I were to go back and examine every single word of the Picuris children's stories, I probably could show you the meaning of anything in the world through their language.

Tiwa words convey a dynamically unfolding reality that is constantly in process. The Tiwa language has no nouns or pronouns, so at Picuris things don't exist as concrete, distinct objects. Everything is a motion and is seen in its relationship to other motions.

For instance, a cup is *tii,* but *tii* likewise means crystallized awareness, or awareness that is in the process of crystallizing and uncrystallizing. That cup is not fixed. In Tiwa it is a continual unfolding of *tii,* and *tii* means "the essence of the power of crystallization that is influencing awareness" and that awareness is the awareness of holding something in, like a spoon, or like tea or coffee. That coffee or tea that is in the cup is not static, either, but it's also in continuous motion.

Of course, "tii" is not a noun or a pronoun, but a verb; therefore, it means not a cup but a cupping, the holding of energy in the process of cupping, and it is cupping another energy that is in the process of being coffee. Everything is a process in relationship with another process.

When I translate Tiwa into English, what I have to do is add the nouns. I have to turn action into nouns. I have to turn relationships into nouns. I have to do that because I am now communicating with people who have nouns and pronouns in their language.

Maybe if you dropped the nouns and pronouns in the English language and just used verbs you'd begin to see the world the way the Tiwa-speaking person sees it — a flow, with everything in motion and relationship to everything else.

All spoken languages play a role in the unfolding of the cosmos. Objectification is part of the map of English, German, or Spanish, but not of many Native American languages.

I believe that the European people came to the Americas for a reason. It wasn't an accident. I don't think there's ever an accident. Europeans, some say, evolved the grid. Because of the fact they evolved the grid, they could accumulate great armies. They can move lots of food and supplies from here to there, and that's their gift to the planet. The Indians, they say, evolved the circle. They can see the complete picture — energies in relationships to other energies. That's where their excellence shows up.

So, maybe that's our role and at the end of time we will see how it all fits together. Each person on the planet in this new century is going to do something that takes the ideas of this time and puts them together, and they'll be just right and it will be good. But we couldn't put it together in the twentieth century because it wasn't our time; it wasn't our job anyway, because that is not what we were doing. We were doing something else.

So, whatever we've contributed, we've contributed. But I

think that there are people out there who, because of what we have contributed, will not have to reinvent the wheel, as they say, but will carry things from there on further and bring humankind to a higher level, a higher consciousness.

Perhaps, before I was twelve I was already preparing myself for my life's work. Then, in 1980, I decided to explore that life's work, and I began actively seeking out visionary experiences and the guidance of Spirit.

VI. LIVING MY VISIONS

The Peace Chambers

AT PICURIS PUEBLO, visions often came in kiva ceremonies. For the Utes, sun dancing is a traditional way of seeking visions.

In July of 1983, I went to take part in the sun dance on the Southern Ute reservation. For three days I fasted, taking no food or water, I danced forward and back and forward again to the center pole.

As I was dancing the vision came of a man standing there looking at me. He moved toward me, then suddenly he disappeared, and where he had been I saw an oval-shaped chamber. Inside that chamber were men and women singing. The chamber was like the little oval music houses I had dreamed about as a seven-year-old child, although I didn't remember that at this time. I did recognize that this chamber was one of those things I'd seen in my vision of the map. It was being revealed to me that this was my next thing to do. Then I had to figure out exactly what was required of me to fulfill this vision.

I asked myself, What is the metaphor here? What is the chamber? What is the human anatomy? What is singing?

Somehow the Vast Self was involved in the sound chamber, not just the individual self. I already knew that what we recognized as the personal self is but an echo of the Vast Self which is the eternal Self. Somehow I knew that the sound chamber had something to do with how the eternal Self was involving all of our lives holistically, and that sound is another form of holism that is an ingredient of our physical well-being, our planetary well-being, our environmental well-being.

Prior to that vision, I had been through a period of maybe five years of semi-madness in which I had a profound urge to move completely into a spiritual realm. I didn't want to get on a street corner and start preaching, I just had this inner determination that I needed to do things that would help bring about a more spiritualized reality.

Once I had the vision of the peace chamber, I started talking about it, and I began looking all over the world for the ideal place to build one.

Months passed. I went looking for a site in Europe and gave lectures there. Then, I went to Virginia Beach before I came home to Bernalillo. I had been gone for a long time — perhaps three months. The second evening after my return people came to a sweat lodge at my home in the trailer park in Bernalillo. People used to come to my house, where I'd give lectures and do ceremonies. They came because I had been able to know things that hadn't happened yet, both personally about individuals and generally about the planet. I didn't know what I was talking about, but I was getting this information in dreams and in visions that I knew were real. They appeared in sharp, vivid color. I had learned that when visions came to me this way, I should not question them, but should just go with what I'd seen. People came to find out about themselves and their problems, and I acquired a reputation for helping them. As soon as I got home from Europe the people came, including Jim Halsey and Minisa Crumbo. We did a sweat lodge that night and during that sweat lodge I had a vision.

Suddenly I was a mile above the earth on some higher plane of existence. Here I saw a group of grandfathers — Native American elders in blankets — sitting in a circle. I walked up to the circle and I knew the council, the place where they were meeting, even though I'd never been there before.

They were expecting me, and they had a question for me. They asked, "Why haven't you built the peace chamber?"

I answered, "I've been looking for the right place, but I haven't found it yet."

One of them said, "Well, we're going to show you where to build it."

The next thing I knew, I found myself standing in the middle of the garden plot in my own back yard in Bernalillo. The circle of elders became a circle of light. This ring of light descended through the night sky and placed itself in my garden, a circle of fire where the walls for the first peace chamber were going to be.

In the next instant I saw a smaller circle of light, no bigger than six feet in diameter. It also descended, and standing on the circle was an angel, about eight feet tall, with curly brown hair, a white robe and wings. He descended, standing on the circle as if he stood on the floor of an elevator. The angel was holding an infant. He came down until his feet touched the ground and then he took the child he was carrying and gently placed it in the ground about two feet under the soil, planting the child like a seed in the center of the circle of light.

The angel never faced me, but as he was standing up, he said to me, "This child is yours to raise." Then he was gone.

Pretty soon I built the first peace chamber there beside my trailer house in Bernalillo.

As a child I was taught that before you began a work that will affect the community, you always go to the elders and ask their approval. You ask if it's OK to undertake this effort. If I were going to build a house, I would go to the elders and they would say, "Yes, you can build a house as long as you stay away from sacred ground. So, we can go and bless your house site." In order to start building sound chambers for world peace, I felt I should go to the United Nations to get their blessing.

In 1987, while in New York, I went with my friend Peggy Owens to the screening of a film sent to the United Nations from the Hopis about the Hopi prophecies. At this event we met an Austrian woman assigned to the United Nations, someone on the staff of the secretary general. I told her about my vision, and that I wanted to present it to the United Nations because I felt this body was the internationally-recognized entity having to do with world peace.

She set up an appointment for me to speak to a UN-sponsored meeting of people who were interested in the paranormal societies. People from all over the world were there, a packed room. To this group I presented the vision I had for the chambers in which to chant in order to promote world peace.

I recounted the vision I'd had about the world peace chambers and that I wanted to build them as I'd seen them in the vision. The people at the UN wrote a letter in support of my work, giving me authority to create the chambers not just in the United States but around the world.

After the first chamber was built, others just began to happen. I started building a second one where I live now in Colorado. Then a third one got established at William Lee Golden's home in Nashville. By the year 2000 there were more than eighty around the world.

The peace (or sound) chambers cannot help but increase. This isn't happening because of good salesmanship. It's just that what's ready to happen is ready to happen.

About five years after I built the chamber in Bernalillo, I was in the chamber getting a massage, when all of a sudden I found myself in an altered state of consciousness. I saw a five-year-old child with brown skin, brown like the land, peeking around the corner of a house at me. Behind the child I saw an elderly man in a white robe with a long beard. Unlike the child, the elderly man was surrounded by a halo of light.

The child asked the elder, "Who's that man lying there on that table."

I was looking directly at the child as he spoke.

The elder, who was the child's guardian, said, "That's your father, your earthly father. You must do whatever he asks you to do."

Then the vision disappeared.

Two years later, I was in the chamber doing a healing ceremony for Minisa's brother when I had another vision. I was shaking red willows over his body when all of a sudden reality changed and I saw that the chamber was sending down roots and ascending upward within the branches of a giant redwood. The redwood tree grew and grew, with the chamber sitting in a fork of its branches, until it had lifted the peace chamber a mile off the ground, to the same plane of existence where I had first spoken with the circle of elders. The child and the ancient guardian were there on that plane as well.

I traveled up there psychically to see where the chamber was. (Physically I was still standing in the peace chamber on the ground). When I arrived in that realm, I saw that there was, on that same plane, a light, moving with the earth's rotation, leaving a band of light like a jet trail as it went. Unlike a jet trail, however, this light never faded. It encircles the earth to this day.

The peace chamber is there is as well, still resting in the branches of the giant redwood, and that chamber looks exactly like the one in my yard in Bernalillo except that it is made entirely of crystals of light.

A Place in Colorado

IT SEEMS as if my visions always were in some ways pro-
phetic; I knew ahead of time that something was going to take
place. Sometimes the images would come three or four days
before the actuality occurred. There wasn't anybody telling me,
"Well, you've got to do this now." I would just get recurring
pictures of something.

In 1980 I was up on the Southern Ute Reservation near
Hesperus, Colorado, and I saw a piece of land at the foot of a
mountain near the La Plata River. The instant I saw that land,
I knew we belonged together. Legally I had no claim to that or
any other land on the reservation. My father had sold my
mother's place in the 1940s. Still, I knew I was supposed to
have that land, so I went to the tribal council and asked for it.
They assigned the land to me, giving me the right to use it for
the rest of my life.

In July of 1983, I was in Colorado on this land, staying
in a camper with my then-wife Maria. One evening, just after
we finished supper, I went outside saying, "I'd really like to see
a flying saucer." At least that's what I remember saying to her.

It was right at dusk, getting dark, and the brightest stars
were quickly appearing. Soon, I knew, we would be able to see
millions of stars in the dry thin air of the Colorado night. As I
looked up at the heavens, suddenly I heard a click in my head,
and the stars leapt closer. It seemed to be happening in me and
through me and outside of me and everywhere. Then there was

a second click and the canopy of stars dropped even closer. Then, with the third click, they got even closer. With the fourth click they were really close, and then I saw eight tiny lights the size of pinheads up against the darkness of the black sky. As they raced across the sky, I knew they were extraterrestrial space craft.

I looked back up and there were four clicks again. With the first click the stars came down; with the second click they came closer. There was a third click and on the fourth click I saw the flying vessels again. When I first saw them they'd been right overhead, but by the second time they were far over to my left, still flying fast.

The next night Maria and I were up where my daughter's house now sits on my land. At that time, I had a trailer house there, and we were standing right by the gate that opened out to the land where we lived. When I looked up, I saw a big space craft hovering about a quarter of a mile above us.

I said, "There's a space ship parked right there." The moment I said it, I saw my thought as red color shooting up toward the craft. When my thought hit, the whole ship rocked. It was about fifteen car lengths long and looked like a long cigar with a bigger front end that tapered off to the back. As my thought hit it, the ship took off going really fast. Then it appeared in physical reality, and for the first time Maria saw it. She said, "Oh, a shooting star."

Finding Oil

ONCE, WHILE we were visiting Maria's family in Tulsa, a man came to see us so I could bless his drum. As we talked, he said, "You know I work for this oil company and we are exploring for new oil, but none of our test wells turns up anything." The man knew I was a shaman and thought I could tell him where to drill for oil.

I had an arrow with me at the time and gave it to him. "Take this arrow and stick it in your back yard. Keep it there for maybe ten days and something will happen."

He said, "OK," and he did it.

He stuck the arrow in the ground, and then he started having dreams. His dreams told him specifically where to drill, in what section of land, in what township.

The man had been on the exploration team, but by the time I met him he had an administrative job in the company. Since he wasn't on the team any longer, he had a hard time getting the people who were now doing exploration for the company to go out and check these spots. Some of these areas had already tested dry. He didn't know how to persuade them, but he would say something like, "Why don't you go over there and test it again just in case it might be something." They hit oil the first time he finally convinced somebody to do that. Then they hit another oil well and another one.

The next time I saw him, about a year later, I said, "How are you doing?"

He said, "You know how I'm doing. We're finding oil where we're not supposed to be finding oil."

Purifying the Oceans

ONE IMPORTANT VISION came to me during early April, 1984. I had gone to Marin County, California, to do a workshop and lectures for the Sufi order. I had just finished leading a sweat lodge there. It had been a really hot sweat and I was lying down next to the lodge to cool off when all of a sudden, three mermen appeared in front of me. The force of their energy pulled me right out of my body. I remember asking the main merman who they were and what was happening. He said, "We're taking you to the being who wants to see you." That was his exact wording. The next thing I knew I was falling off the side of a cliff into the ocean.

As I was falling, I looked down and I saw three little white splashes, where the three mermen had dived into the ocean. I followed, falling down into the water, pulled by the mermen's energy. I saw one of the mermen in front of me then, and I was pulled after him.

We went into an underwater cavern, through a corridor, and then up into a vast cavern under the ocean floor.

The next thing I knew I was standing in front of a beautiful Being who wore a metallic blue cape. He sat on a jewel-studded throne, a majestic presence with a bright pink face. From his whole being, he emanated a deep, loving presence. He was looking down at me, and he said, "I want you to build a fire on the seventh of April, and I want you to build that fire for me. I want you to build it because that fire is going to purify the oceans."

Then the vision disappeared and I found myself trying to get back into my body outside the sweat lodge.

Coincidentally, as I was lying there emerging from this experience, a man came up to me and said, "Sir, I'm lost. I'm trying to get back to the city." He looked at me again and said, "Joseph, is that you?" It was a man whom I'd been counseling back in New Mexico. He was a recovering alcoholic, in California looking for a job.

"This is amazing," he told me. "I've just been thinking about you, missing you, so I took a drive out in the country and got lost. I saw the fire here and I came to get directions."

Another vision occurred a few days later. I was driving on Colorado State Road 122 near the LaPlata River in southwestern Colorado when I saw a shark swimming across the dirt road in front of the car. "I just saw a shark swim by," I said to Dr. Houghton, a psychiatrist, who was sitting next to me in the car. He looked at me and said, mostly from habit, "Are you all right?"

"Yes," I answered in an unusually high-pitched voice, surprising myself by the way I answered. Again, I said, "See there it goes again," as it crossed back over in front of my car. Then it disappeared. We continued on to my land in Kline, Colorado, and built a fire for healing my land. As we camped out overnight, we took some pictures of the fire. The next day we drove to my home in Bernalillo.

Two weeks later we were all gathered in the Bernalillo peace chamber when Dr. Houghton spotted some color snapshots on a table. "Are these the pictures we took of the fire two weeks ago?"

"Yes."

"Say," said Dr. Houghton, "I see a shark behind the fire in this photograph."

"That makes sense," I said. "Remember that a shark was following us that day on the road."

In 1987 I was in Findhorn, Scotland, leading a workshop, and there was talk at the center at Findhorn (which is near the sea) that companies were dumping industrial waste into the ocean, polluting it so much that the dolphins had left. The people there asked me, "What can we do?"

I said, "Let's just go down there now."

We walked down to the beach and we built a fire there on the sand. Once the fire was going I gave them a sound to chant to the ocean. By this time I had a track record with oceans, so this ceremony was not out of the ordinary for me. I had been building fires in the peace chamber on the seventh of every month since my vision of the mermen in 1984.

We started chanting and about four minutes into the chanting, a little baby, six months old, who was there in his mother's arms, started making strange sounds.

The mother came up to me with him and said, "What's going on? Why is my son making these sounds?"

At that moment, I realized that he was making dolphin sounds; he was picking up what the dolphins were saying to us and verbalizing it. Through this baby, the dolphins were acknowledging us, letting us know they had received the blessings we were sending by chanting.

Paying Back the Lions

ONE DAY I WENT HUNTING up on the mountain with Agapito Martinez's brother, Pat. He took the lower trail, and I took the upper trail, and we hunted all day. We were supposed to meet at six o'clock back down where we had left my truck.

About midday I saw two deer coming out of the brush. I shot one of them, which went down, and the other one ran off. When I went to the deer I'd shot, suddenly I walked into a vibrational energy that was different from any I had ever experienced before. I heard a loud, clear voice saying to me, "Don't touch the deer. If you want to bless it with cornmeal, you just bless it around the ears."

So, I said, "OK. I won't bother it." I blessed it, sprinkling cornmeal around its ears. I felt terrible about leaving the meat there, but I left and returned to meet Pat Martinez at the truck.

He finally arrived, and he asked, "Did you shoot?"

I said, "Yes, I shot at one and it got away." I didn't want to tell him that I had left the meat up there.

Then he said, "Let me tell you a story. One winter in the 1930s, the village was very hungry. Your godfather and I came up here hunting. We went up that ridge where you were and we shot a deer. It was getting late in the evening, too late to follow the blood that was coming from the wounded deer, so we came down right here where this river is. There were two lions here. They were burying something, and we saw them. It was late in the evening and very cold. When we went to see what the lions had hidden, there was a carcass of a deer just barely eaten. So, we put it on the back of the mule, and we started carrying it down to the village.

"As we were carrying it down, your godfather started joking. He said, 'It looks like we're carrying a wooden cross.' The name of the mountain where we had been hunting that day was Wooden Cross Mountain."

Pat didn't know what he was telling me, but I was beginning to get suspicious. I realized that he didn't know that I'd left the deer up there. Now I suspected I'd been instructed to leave the deer meat up there to pay the mountain lions back for the deer our village took from them all those decades ago.

Three days later I went to Tulsa, where I met Jim Halsey, who invited me to his house in Independence, Kansas. He and I drove from Tulsa to Independence. When we got there, Minisa was in the kitchen cooking dinner and talking to a guest. The guest said to her, "Should I give it to him?" I thought he was going to give me some tobacco, because that's the customary gift for a medicine man.

Instead, he gave me a lion's paw. He said, "I used to live in Taos, and I understand that this mountain lion was harvested on Wooden Cross Mountain. I brought this to you because I had a dream two or three days ago when I talked to Minisa. I had a dream and in that dream, I was told I was supposed to bring this to you. So, here it is."

This kind of thing has occurred time and again in my life, and I suspect I'm not the only person to whom such things happen. I suspect other people, those who live by faith, are continually being caught by surprise and are having great experiences with the supernatural — being lucky, getting gifts because of effort. Once the supernatural beings realize who you are and you get in a relationship with them, you can't get away from them no matter how hard you try.

VII. SHARING THE CEREMONIES

Giving and Receiving

IN 1980 I started leading long dances in which both Indian and non-Indian people participated. Typically, the groups would gather out on my land or somebody else's and we'd do a sweat lodge ceremony, after which I would talk to them about the dance. Then, usually with somebody drumming for us, we would walk or dance in a big circle all night long.

Later, on a few occasions, I led thunder-calling or rain-calling ceremonies. In 1986, I started leading drum dances, then in 1987 I began to lead sun/moon dances for groups all over the world. Many of these dances and ceremonies are still being held, though I rarely lead them any more. In 1999 I retired and turned over the leadership of most of the dances to people I had trained.

The ceremonies I did were based, philosophically, on the teachings I had at Picuris and on the Southern Ute reservation, but in the end, the present moment decided what I would do to bring the supernatural powers into that moment. I don't think I've ever really followed the method that was taught to me at Picuris to call the rain, for instance. I learned that method, but I've never actually followed it, not even one time. Once I have tobacco in my hand and I'm going to offer it for some help to make it rain, then I open myself up to that moment. I don't have to know a ceremony beforehand. The moment determines what that ceremony is going to be.

Many Indians have a problem with sharing these ceremonies with non-Indians. I think it is because they haven't shared them in the past, because it wasn't yet time for them to do so. Even the Indians didn't know that they were supposed to hold them until such time as the ceremonies were ready to come forth. A ceremony is like a child that belongs to the tribe. Now they have to share that ceremony because the time has come for the child to go out into the world.

To give is to receive. In order to keep a thing, we have to give it away. When we keep something for too long and don't share it, the soul of the keeper begins to die because there's no movement. There's no emotional, physical, spiritual movement in the psyche of that moment for that person, for that tribe. Tribalism comes with a mandate, and that mandate is to give to the larger whole.

But when we share what we have, we begin to move energy in ourselves, and we begin to grow spiritually. Then the supernatural powers begin to open up for the giver. The supernatural powers are the gifts that come in the giveaway. I think St. Francis of Assisi knew that. When he presented his prayer to the church, he said, "To give is to receive" and "It is in death that we have eternal life."

Supernatural powers come to us when we give what we have kept over the years. Now it is time. This esoteric teaching is ready to be given out. What we need most in the world today is a great deal of supernatural support. I don't think we have it now in the way that we used to because we have become too crystallized. We've become too stuck in form. We've put a high value on form, and we think the form is what makes a thing work.

Maybe we have gotten too caught up in technology and now is the time that technology has reached its highest potential. Now it's time for us to reawaken and move to the total opposite of technology where we rely on the supernatural powers that were here before we came to inhabit the earth. So, if I want to fly across a railroad early in the morning as I once saw a Navajo medicine man do, or if I want to have telescopic sight, or if I want to be able to disappear and reappear in another place randomly, now is the time. Over time everything becomes its opposite. Now is the time for the opposite to happen. That way technology can be complemented by the No-form.

Now is the time to change our relationship, not just to technology, but also to money.

Several years ago my publisher sent a friend of hers to me for counseling because she was having problems with her finances. I gave her friend $100 and told her to give it to anyone on the street, whomever she wanted. So, she went out and she gave it to someone. Soon after that she got a good job with a big salary. Now my publisher, being nice and wanting me to know that I was her friend, gave me a $100 check. She told me to spend it on a certain slot machine at the casino. I went and put it in the slot machine and I won $2,500. That's what happens with me and money, you see.

During the years I was leading ceremonies, I always made money, but I didn't have time to spend it because I was always re-investing it in more dances, more peace chambers. I was expanding my work. I'd send money to build the foundation of a chamber or to build a corral for the dances. Now all that money is starting to come back in from different sources, mostly sources unrelated to my work.

Back when I was working, I was supposed to accumulate a lot of money, but I've found that money never comes to me the way it is supposed to.

The Tiwa word to explain this is *wee-who*. It means that when you give, expect nothing in return. Just don't even think about it.

But what is giving? When you give, you open yourself to a primal landscape of the psyche — a primal area that's fully evolved with the high density of resonances that are just pulsating with high levels of energy. When you give, you open that corridor of energy for yourself and your kind or your people, your vibrations, and it is filled with goodness — greatness that has the power of awareness within it so that it descends upon you and places in you whatever that gift is that you are supposed to get. That's what giving does. It awakens place-ment. It brings down clarity, and clarity and placement attract money, because money also wants to find a place for itself.

In Tiwa, *wee* means "to give" and *who* is "the higher power that makes it happen." When we give we bring together greatness, awareness and placement; the result is that we open a channel to up-above. This is because the gifts come from up-above, not from down-below. It's like a computer program. All it knows is that when you put side-by-side the power of great-ness, the power of awareness, and the power of placement on this flat surface, and you combine those and open the channel to the higher planes — which is what happens when you give — then the universe throws something in through that pipe and it comes down to you as a gift in return for giving. It's usually ten-fold what you gave.

Any time we give we receive. As soon as we're born here on earth, we're born giving ourselves to this world. So, from the time we're little children until the time we're adults, all we're doing throughout life is giving. We're giving of ourselves because we're not really from here anyway. We're here on loan from some other place. We gave this time so we could be here to do whatever we're doing here.

In doing ceremony, no matter what the ceremony, we're honoring the four directions. We're honoring the four direc-tions because we are the four directions. When we honor the east which is the mental, the south which is the emotional, the west which is the physical and the north which is the spiritual, we're honoring our own physical bodies, mental bodies, emotional bodies, and spiritual bodies. So, when you go into the sweat lodge and you pray to the four directions, you're also praying for your own directions, which are to the north, to the south, to the east, to the west. Also, you are praying in compliance with the cosmos, which, like you, has the north, the south, the east, the west, the up above and the down below.

I found out over the years that people who come in from western thought don't understand about donation. They think donation is whatever you can give and that's fine. What I understand about donation is this: The more you give, the more you get in return. So, if you give $500 for ceremony, you're going to get something worth $20,000 back. If you put $10 or $30, then that determines what you are going to get in return. In terms of effort, the more you put in, the more you get back. The more effort you put in, the more you get back. If we can get people to start thinking that and believing more from the place of faith, it will have a powerful impact on our world. Apply some effort in your life and then rely on faith. Have faith that it will be returned to you, as opposed to what all of us have done in the past, which is make a donation then keep a receipt for a tax deduction.

That's OK for a while, but this other works even better. The main thing that happens when you rely on faith is that you learn some very interesting things about trust. Until we can trust ourselves and our relationship to life, we can't really trust others or trust situations. We're always afraid of losing out. We are trained to go see a lawyer when we create something, because we want everything in black and white. I know a lot about that because I worked with federal guidelines when I was working with the tribes. Everything had to be written in black and white — paperwork. I understand all of that, and I understand the reason for it, and it's good. But we lose the other potential possibilities when we stick to the straight and narrow and all those legal things that we have to do to keep it written down.

We lose the ability of just saying, "I'm going to give money to my publisher's friend and tell her to give it to a stranger." I didn't say to her, "Give it back to me." I didn't say, "Well, you can pay me back whenever you can. It's a lot of money to loan to you. I don't think I should be doing this, but I like it." No, I didn't set any limitation. I said, "Here, just go do it." In hindsight, I could have used the $100, but I also knew that was my contribution to her life, and that was what was important. Then one day it resolved itself and I got back $2,500.

The European who taught this truth about giving was St. Francis of Assisi. While I was leading sun/moon dances all over Europe, I brought the Austrians who had been dancing with me, and the Germans, the English, the Irish, the Scots, the Italians — all those people from those different countries — to Assisi to dance with me. In fact, the dance site overlooked the church that was dedicated to St. Francis. You could see it from our dance ground. I wanted to dance the sun/moon dance where St. Francis of Assisi had walked because he believed that to give is to receive.

They are still doing sun/moon dances in Assisi.

While in Assisi, I visited the tomb of St. Francis, and I remembered again the whole philosophy of giving. That's what I was taught as a child, and it's what I've seen hold true in my life. After years of doing all the spiritual work and giving back almost all of what I earned to that work, I retired, not knowing how I could afford to live. Then, the Southern Ute tribe came around and offered me a retirement check for the rest of my life, which was unexpected. Some might say I would have received a pension from the Southern Utes anyway, but I think I was given retirement security because of my spiritual work.

Origins of the Picuris

IN 1989, while I was in Pennsylvania, I had a vision about the origins of Picuris. In the vision, I was up in the sky looking down through a hole at the earth. All I saw was a big mud flat, no mountains or valleys. All of a sudden, I saw what looked like a ship come down and land. Two kachinas got out and then they turned into vibrations. They began to vibrate that whole mud flat. I realized that I was seeing a time, eons ago, when the oceans had just receded in North America. Then I saw changes happening on the earth — happening quickly, like pages turning in a book. I saw the landscapes of Picuris changing again and again, until finally there was vegetation, and then there was the river, and finally there was land, then there were mountains and trees. Maybe thousands of years went by, until I saw my grandmother's house, and outside where the ship had landed were the Blue Stones, which Picuris calls the Blue Stone People.

I found myself southwest of Picuris and I saw that there was a crack in the earth. To the left of that crack, sixteen people appeared spontaneously. They came out of nothing into something, and they had human forms. There were little children, adults, grandmothers and grandfathers, and some of the men had bows and arrows with them.

In the eighth or ninth grade I read a geography book that explained several different theories about matter. One of the theories is that energy comes together to form matter. It's not in material form yet, but it comes together and keeps getting more and more centralized and more and more accumulative. Then, all of a sudden, when it reaches a certain solidity, it explodes into being. That's what I saw in my vision.

I don't think the Picuris people came from anywhere else on earth. This is what I saw, and this is what I believe. For me, they just came out of nothing into something. They came southwest of Picuris, but at a time when Picuris was not there yet. There was no village when the people originally went to Picuris. Just the landscape. In my vision I saw these people appear spontaneously out of nothing into something from the crack in the earth.

It was as if the two kachinas had seeded the land with

energy. I saw their bodies change into, and become, lights spreading out over the physical landscape of what was to become the village of Picuris Pueblo, New Mexico.

When I talk of outer space and kachinas coming in ships, it doesn't mean that the Tiwa people belong to another planet or that the kachinas came from another solar system. That's not what I'm saying at all. I'm saying that there were outside energies that came into this perceptual reality, and those energies manifested to me as kachinas who were black and white.

Black is "divine breath" and white is "the power to change" so the black gives life because it's the breath. The white is the perceptual reality, but because it's perceptual, it's always in a state of impermanence. The black and white stripes of the kachinas show we are born out of nothing into a world of variety and change.

When the Picuris people ate from the plants that were there in that landscape, they understood their language, the language of metaphor. The language gave them their particular understanding of reality. It was already innate in that resonating vibration of the land. So, they naturally just became speakers of the land, and they spoke in the Tiwa language from that moment on.

When I was a child, everybody in Picuris spoke Tiwa. It was required of us to speak, and we never even thought about learning it. We learned to speak Tiwa by letting the words that were being spoken bounce off of our faces. The eyes digested them, the nose expanded the meaning of the words spoken, the skin on our faces grasped their meaning and our ears gave us the structure to use the words appropriately.

So, when I was studying Tiwa, and I have been studying Tiwa all my life, the first thing I learned was that it is not a language based on logic or a particular philosophy. It's a language based on the resonating vibration of the land and what comes out of the land, like the trees, like the river. The river is named after the sound that the river makes. Wood is named after the sound that wood makes. The words used for walking, or for land, or for tree, are all based on the way that these things sound. So, if you say *tii-e-moo* (that's for cup), if you listen, you can hear a cup. The land calls paper *tuh uh nay,* and if you listen to the sound a piece of paper makes as you pick it up, you hear *tuh uh nay.*

It's already natural for the human body to speak Tiwa. When I teach about the language of the land, I'm not saying that you have to learn anything new about who you are. If we are the land — and I believe we are the land — then we already come equipped with knowledge of how to speak in words through our mouths, and how to speak genetically. We manifest according to the grammar of our genes; our genetic structure is the language of the resonating vibration of our ancestors.

The power in the Tiwa language is not so much in the words themselves but in the sounds that are made in pronouncing the words.

It is the same with English. Put your hand on a flat surface like a tabletop, and you'll hear the word "flat." The sound of flatness came first and then came the creative energies that patterned the flat surfaces on places. Shapes, surfaces are not really stationary but are constantly in a state of flow. There are no objects, really, only processes and relationships.

Spoken words are constantly creating our universes because we are essences of perpetuity. Everything on the earth since the beginning of time has been and is being created by the sounds of words as they are spoken.

In trance state I saw that we are made of numbers and words. Vibration is what makes the numbers possible. Vibration is energy that is descending and crystallizing itself so that it can then become active, and once it becomes active, then it becomes a radiance. It shoots out the light of its presence in that instant. The energy is measured in waves of light or numbers, lines and squares, and geometry. Everything is made of the vibrations of numbers and spoken words.

Turning Visions into Art

AS A YOUNG TEENAGER at the Santa Fe Indian School I was given some brushes and was taught how to mix colors by Ray Toledo. One day he was walking down the aisle in the art class and he looked at my work. He told me that I had a direct pipeline to God and that when I drew I was drawing images that were coming from the inner source, from the spiritual place. He said, "You know, you're going to be an artist. You're going to be a good one, but the images that you draw are going to be coming from that place where all things come from."

I didn't know what he meant. In fact, two minutes later I forgot what he said. All I knew was that from his smile, he liked what I was doing. Years later, when I went to work at the Santa Fe Indian Hospital, a medical anthropologist working on her Ph.D. dissertation came from New Jersey to interview Indian artists. She wanted to show in some way that Indians were actually drawing from the spiritual realm. That's where they were getting their ideas. She was stationed at the hospital where a doctor was supervising her.

She and I didn't get along very well, because she thought I was a fake. She envisioned native artists who had never been educated in a white man's world. Somehow the spiritual realm put us together at the Santa Fe Indian hospital. Another lady working with her was one of my good friends, a Vista worker.

I had been drawing and painting again, so one day after the anthropologist had been there maybe a year, she came to me and said she had decided to interview me.

As she started talking about the theory she was developing, I agreed with her and told her about some of my experiences. She got upset with me because she thought I was either making it up or just trying to agree with her.

As we spoke, my body started getting hotter and hotter and hotter, and I knew I was in trouble because when that happens, the power of the supernatural comes through. It doesn't happen very often. I'm not afraid of it, but I know that I can't control it. It's not me; it's another presence that comes through. It's a presence that has a hard time staying in this body, as if it's vibrating at fifty megacycles to my twenty-five, vibrating in every single cell in my body. It's not a fun state for me, but what comes in is a very high, very intelligent presence.

This presence came into me during the interview with that lady. My face began changing, and I became a woman, a grandmother. I could see my face because I also became another being right there where she was standing. The anthropologist stared at me; her eyes kept getting bigger. I spoke to her, or rather the presence did, and it turned out it was her aunt who had died about five years before.

The presence said something like, "You don't believe anything, do you? You don't even believe your auntie over here."

Then I started coming back into my body. I heard everything, I saw everything, but I came from fifty megacycles down to twenty-five again. It happened really, really fast.

The other woman, my friend, happened to be in the room during this interview. As the vibration was slowing down, I could hear her saying to the anthropologist, "You went to all the Indian reservations and you talked to all the Indian artists. The last person you came to see had what you were looking for all the time."

I didn't know it at the time, but there had been contention between the anthropologist and her aunt. Now she had the entire conversation on tape and reported it in her paper.

I have done artwork off and on through the years, but since about 1990 I've been spending more time on it and have started showing and selling my work.

Painting is a form of meditation for me, a way to connect with the higher source. Painting is one way I do medicine. After I've been drawing, I feel the way I think people feel when they've been to the confessional, or when they receive the holy communion. I feel the way people feel when there's been some catharsis. That's what happens when I draw.

I may have some idea of what I want to do, but when the drawing starts, I know that my hands are being guided and my ideas are coming together on the canvas or on the paper. I may not understand why they are coming through, but they are usually connected to some source of power or some combination of words that came out of the Picuris children's stories, or the everyday language that the Picuris spoke in the 1940s when I was learning how to speak Tiwa.

When I do artwork, I start with an idea. For instance I'm in bed and I get an idea that I want to draw a horse running. Then, as I'm drawing the idea keeps changing until eventually I'll get an image that I didn't really start with. I may draw an image of a horse, but some other things will be included which will end up really emphasizing some spiritual principle.

People look at my art and ask, "Well, is this Picuris art?" I'll say, "Yeah, in a way it is."

It's Picuris because my childhood language was Tiwa, and

I was taught the Picuris children's stories and principal ideas about the supernatural world. If that's what you mean, that's Picuris, but the actual images came through in the process of painting and I didn't even know that's what was going to turn out. It's just my art, coming from Source. My art is Picuris because I am, but not for any other reason. After a while, I began to see that is this also happening to English-speaking people. Our language creates our world view and our art.

Conversing with the Dead

ONE OF THE GIFTS I have received for whatever reason is the ability to cross over from the everyday plane of existence into other planes. Several times during my life, I have had contact with people who have died. My Aunt Carmelita, my father's sister, died in the 1970s. I went with my wife at the time, Ruth, to the Hood Mortuary in Durango where Carmelita's body lay in state, to pay my respects and pray. While I was there, I took an eagle feather and laid it across her hands. The instant I did this, one of the candles near her coffin popped and caught the rug in front of the coffin on fire.

We quickly put out the fire, but I knew it was Carmelita who had caused this to happen. Whatever she did, she was having a good time.

The next morning we came back to the mortuary, but the body had already been taken to the Catholic church. Ruth and I went to the church, and we sat down on a pew toward the back because we were late.

At that point, I happened to look up, and there was Carmelita with her son Faustin Tucson, who had died some time before her. I saw them plain as day above us. Carmelita communicated to me telepathically and said, "We're all right. We're fine. We're leaving now." They disappeared, and then after that all I could see was the ceiling of the church.

My foster mother was Catholic, and when she died, a rosary was held for her at her house. I always had trouble going to funerals or going to rosaries when people died because I had resisted saying goodbye to my mother when she died. But this was one rosary I had to go to. Again, I came in after everybody was already praying, and I kneeled down. It wasn't long before I felt excruciating pain in my knees. Still, I knelt there trying to be proper and trying to pray with everyone else and trying not to feel out of place or disturb what was going on. I kept fidgeting to find a better position for my knees, but I couldn't. Then all of a sudden, I saw there was a white light coming from the heads of all of these people.

I looked up and my foster mother was standing there with my foster father who had died a few years before her. They stood in front of me, holding hands. Again, they communicated to me that they were all right, and I saw them float across the top of the heads of the people in the room. They went to my left, and then they started traveling south.

I closed my eyes, and I could follow them, watching their backs. They went farther and farther and they kept going until they came to the place where the Picuris teachings say the Picuris people go after they die. It is on the side of a mountain. When my foster parents got there, the side of the mountain opened up, and I could see some of the people from Picuris who had died years before, whom I remembered from my childhood. All these people came and met my foster parents. They went through the tunnel to the Other Side, and it closed and I saw just the mountain there. Then I was back in my body, back in the room.

During a sun dance I saw another person who had died. George Durand was from Picuris Pueblo and we were boyhood friends. Later, in about 1954, he was stationed at Fort Bliss, Texas, where they were working with the Sidewinder Missiles that were being tested at White Sands Missile Range in New Mexico. He had a 1947 Chevy, and when he came home on weekends we'd ride around in it. Then, in 1979, he died.

It was 1983 when I saw George again. I was on the Southern Ute Reservation lying down in a sleeping bag at the sun dance. I had been dancing for two days with no food or water, and I was resting. All of a sudden, I felt a presence to my left. I looked over, and he was sitting there just as clear as any person in the flesh. I said to him, "What are you doing here?" It didn't even occur to me at first that he had died. I had forgotten that. I was just surprised he had come to this sun dance, two hundred miles from Picuris, in Ignacio.

He said, "Well, I'm here. I'm just keeping you company because I know you are going through a hard time."

"Yeah," I replied, "I'm going through a lot of struggle with no food, no water."

"I'm going to take you somewhere, where you can have some food," he told me. "Bet you're hungry."

I left my physical body and in my etheric body I went with him. We crossed the dance ground and then another dimension opened. Here on a long table were all kinds of fruits, watermelons, and an abundance of food.

"Why are you doing this?" I asked.

He said, "Well, because when you sit down to eat, you always feed us symbolically in your prayers. You have never forgotten to pray for the dead."

It's true. When I eat, I will feed the dead. It's a custom a lot of native people follow. You take some of the food with your left hand and you drop it on the floor or the ground. Before you eat, you always feed the dead, all those people who have gone before. Because I had done this, he told me I could eat there.

I invited him to eat with me. I said, "You want to eat?"

"No."

"Why not?"

"Because we don't eat here, but you can eat if you want." So, I just started eating because I was hungry.

Then, I came back into my body on the sleeping bag inside the circle where we were doing the sun dance. For the next day or so, my body functioned as if I had eaten a big meal.

I also saw my father after he died, with Carmelita, his sister. They were going from one building to the next. They were basically ignoring me because they were onto something. They were aware of my presence there, but they didn't stop to talk to me because they were involved in a different reality. There are different realities that are going on simultaneously in addition to this one.

In the vision at the sun dance, I saw George Duran, and also other people from Picuris standing in a field with hoes, like garden hoes. This is how I saw them. They were hoeing the land and preparing it for seeding. The land had already been plowed, tilled and planed so it was ready to be seeded. But they were not planting corn or peas or beans as they used to do here. They were seeding new eternities, planting other realities.

I asked them, "What are these new worlds going to look like?"

They said, "That's not up for discussion."

I noticed that thing about my teachers at Picuris, too. You never could ask them questions or expect to get answers from them because they said that it was not up to them to give you answers. The reason that they didn't give you answers is because they didn't want you to get stuck believing that they had the answers and therefore you had to go to them. They wanted you to learn that the answers have to come from within yourself. Any time you ask a question, you already have the answer. Whether you want to believe it or not, of course, is your problem, not theirs. That's one of the teachings.

The other thing they did at Picuris was to avoid teaching any forms or religious practices because they said if you do that, you get stuck in those forms. By and large, you don't get beyond them.

There were some rituals that we all took part in as a result of thankfulness for life, and that was all right, but we were taught not to get stuck in these other forms because they are not real. In other words, if I felt like I wanted to make a dance to the apple tree, because it provides apples for the family, that kind of ceremony was all right, or to do a deer dance, or a buffalo dance. The apple is really not an apple. It is a metaphor for an archetype, just as the deer is a metaphor for an archetype. But it was important not to get stuck in any ceremonial form. I was taught to keep as limited as possible any form that I used to worship or to help others worship.

I believe the Tiwa-speaking people lived in the wilderness on purpose. Today, we in the United States have a lot of technology so we have to build things in order to maintain that technology. We have to mine iron ore to make steel for instance, so that we can build a building that is called a factory where we make cars, or where we refine steel. We have all these other things that we put on the earth as a result of technologies that we need and have to create. Therefore, we are stuck in these technological forms. What the Picuris elders were saying was not to get stuck in any particular form. We don't really need telephones and cars. We can rely on supernatural powers to communicate telepathically. We can teleport if we choose to.

We can use other forms. If we start relying too much on materialism, then we start cluttering up the land which is really the Self, the infinite Self, which is also us.

I had an insight that the diseases presently on the planet — and we have always had diseases on the planet — are a way in which the earth can heal itself. By carrying illnesses, we heal the planet. The planet is a metaphor for the Self, or for a combination of archetypes, which is *paa ah nay*. *Paa* — "in the direction of" — is one archetype, *ah* — "in the clarity of that direction" — is another, and *nay* — "how the Self is placing itself" — is the third. It takes three archetypes to make the metaphor that in fact becomes a round planet, this round planet we call Planet Earth, and the plants, animals, and things that grow on it. So what they used to say is that if you want to keep in line with piety, or with greatness, or with sacredness, you have to stay within those guidelines of *paa ah nay*. When they say *paa ah nay* they are talking about the people, not just the human people, but the plant people, the tree people, the ocean people, the river people, because "people" means "vibration."

In all these experiences of seeing people who have died, it has always seemed that there is no room for remembering their death, or even that they died. It is as if they have always been there. This is my experience. Apparently, when we die, we are no longer physically here, but we are here; we're just not in the same form. In fact, we're not perceivable as we perceive the material plane, but other than that, apparently, we are still here.

I think maybe you and I are already there in those other realms as well. We exist simultaneously in this physical, perceptual realm and in other realities. Right now we are in these physical forms which bring together several realms. One realm is just the fingernail archetype. One is just the skin archetype of reality. Here we have the combination. We have fingernails, skin, hands, a heart. All those are separate realities. Here in this reality they are all are put together.

It's not that those realities are less complete than this one, it's just that they're each doing their own thing. They're holding themselves. They're totally complete in themselves. Over here, we get to wear the whole suit. In other words, if I am an eye and I am in that other reality, I know all the other parts, but I am just experiencing that one part.

I am held in the pattern of being an eye, but in some place, there is still a form of me — my emotional body, my spiritual body, my energetic body — that is simultaneously here but also in a finer vibrational form connected to, I hope, the other beings who have a finer vibration.

We don't exist. So, if we think we exist, we are already in trouble. And I'm in trouble now because I am trying to explain something that doesn't exist.

An eye exists, skin exists, the different forms exist, but they don't exist in the way that we think they exist. They have a finer vibrational form than that of this reality.

So, since we don't exist, we appear and disappear, not only in this realm but in all the other realms. We are doing the whole enchilada, but in any given moment, we are only experiencing that moment, that reality.

My sister-in-law Lorencita Simbola died recently. She had diabetes, was an amputee, and suffered for many years. When she died, I was outside hanging clothes, and I had put a candle in the sound chamber, when all of a sudden, I felt her presence very near. Then I knew she was present in that moment when I was hanging clothes. It was about one o'clock in the afternoon.

I could clearly hear her thoughts saying to me, "I was a diabetic because that was the way I was purifying myself. That was what I needed. Now I am free, and I don't have to come back here to do this over again. I'm free."

Another thing happened at the same time that she was telling me that. Everything turned golden — there was gold light everywhere. I could see the house and I looked over toward the water truck that was sitting nearby. I could see the truck through the golden light that was everywhere in the air.

She said, "That's what it's like here. It's really beautiful, and I don't hurt any more."

The gold lasted another three minutes, then it faded away, and everything was normal again.

Illness is an opportunity to deal with some imbalance for the planet. Or, since the planet is also part of the galaxies, and since it is also part of all of the solar systems, perhaps we are dealing with it for some other planet, like the woman who died at Picuris and everybody feasted for three days in her honor.

The holy men said that she had been carrying something from some other solar system way on the other side of the cosmos, and that was what her illness was about. It wasn't from here. They taught that over there is also over here, because it's all one.

Calling in the Thunder

YEARS after my boyhood initiation as a Picuris Thunder-caller, in July of 1991, I did a thunder-calling ceremony in Colorado. I think the last one I had participated in had been in when I was my teens.

I had always had the idea that my ceremonies, such as the thunder calling, would work only at Picuris because of the land there. By 1990, I was just beginning to understand that there is an omnipresence anywhere on the earth, and if my instincts were to do a ceremony, I needed to do it. A powerful inner force was asking me do to a thunder-calling ceremony near my house in Colorado. I invited people to come to see it because that was what the ceremony was calling for. By this time I had been out of high school almost forty years, and I didn't have the clan around me to do the ceremony with. I had no official or ceremonial position with either the Southern Ute tribe of my mother or the pueblo of my father. I was on my own. So it was under no authority except my own that I determined after thirty-nine years of not doing the ceremony I'd learned as a youth that I was going to do the thunder-calling ceremony on my land in Colorado the following July.

In January of 1991 I asked the spirits to help me make it rain the following July. I asked in January because you have to ask at the beginning of the year. I don't know why we have to ask for rain in January, but that's the way I was taught. So I asked in January of 1991 for help to make it rain the following summer. We believe that the people who help us bring the rain are relatives who have died. For instance, if my grandmother had died in January, she would probably show up sometime in July and help me do the thunder-calling ceremony. So, I asked for any relatives who wanted to help to come.

Six months later, on July 9, I had gathered a group of people, mostly non-Indians, at my place. The next day we were going to do the thunder-calling ceremony, but I still hadn't gotten confirmation about who was going to help me bring in the rain. The night before the ceremony I went to sleep, and soon after my head hit the pillow, I had a dream. In the dream my deceased foster parents, Lucia and Agapito Martinez, showed up. They had been dead for over ten years, and it was good to see them in spirit. They were all dressed up in their Indian regalia as if they were going to a feast.

When I had lived with my foster parents as an older child and teenager, my foster mother felt she needed to make sure I kept my appointments. Some of the elders would come over, and say, "Joseph, we're going to do a ceremony three days from now. We want you to come over and dance with us." I'd always forget, and my foster mother would remind me, "Joseph, you remember you have to go to that ceremony over there."

Now, almost forty years later, my foster parents showed up in my dream, all dressed up. My foster mother was in her nineties when she died, I think, but she looked more like forty-five in this dream. My foster father, Agapito Martinez, looked younger, too. I was in the room with them and I remember asking them, "What are you all dressed up for?"

My foster mother said, "Joseph, you haven't changed. You're still forgetting what you're supposed to do. I guess I have to come here to remind you again. You're doing a ceremony tomorrow to bring in the thunder." Of course, she was talking to me in Tiwa.

I said, "Oh yeah, I remember."

"Well, we're here to tell you. We're going to be there at exactly two o'clock tomorrow, in the afternoon." Then, of course, they disappeared.

The day of the ceremony dawned sunny and clear, with no hint of rain in the forecast. But I had learned as a boy not to question my foster parents' instructions, just to follow them. So, I gathered everyone and said, "I'm going to line you up over here. We're going to take these stones, and we're going to start lifting them up to the sky and back down; up to the sky and back down, slowly."

This was something I had learned from my grandfather

when I was twelve. He had died by then, and he would come to teach me in my dreams while I was at the Santa Fe Indian School.

Following what he taught me, I knew we had to get the stones from the river. You can't just pick them anywhere. They have to be river rocks. After the ceremony was over, most of the people wanted to take the rocks home. I said, "You can't take them. You have to put them back in the river because they're the Water People."

At least twenty of my students were attending the ceremony, including Tom and Kristen Bissinger, Sherry Boatright, Geri and Gary Gibbons from Hesperus, Colorado, Ellen Lyngstad from Norway, John Morrison, Bonnie Penna, Angie Rapalyea, Russell P. Robertson, Lois Burwell from England, India Isherwood, Mary Elizabeth Marlow, Patricia O Casey, Carolyn Powell, Ken Rich from New York, Barbara Vanderhoff, and Gerd Bjørke from Norway. Of these, there were eight people that I chose — four men and four women — to do the ceremony. There were no clouds in the sky. But I started the eight people lifting the stones and lowering them slowly.

Right at two o'clock low, rolling thunder drummed across the sky. We could hear it getting louder and louder, even though there were still no clouds in sight. After that first roll of thunder, I started the prayers, but I would break every three or four minutes. Whenever I stopped, and only when I stopped, there would be another roll of thunder. What's interesting about thunder beings is that they are very polite and they don't break in when you are talking. They wait until the prayer ends and then you hear them.

The thunder kept coming and I kept praying aloud because you have to pray for all of the directions. You have to pray for the insect community and you have to pray for all of life — the two-leggeds, the four-leggeds.

Soon it started to rain. It was the soft rain, the Father Sun rain that makes awareness — that irrigates the inner recesses of the Vast Soul.

We could look up and see rain, a circle of silver rain about twenty feet in diameter, and it was falling on us like light snow, weightless drops of water, but there were no clouds in the sky yet. There was a bright afternoon sun, and we could see the water coming down, right at us.

Here is what one of the participants in that ceremony remembers:

The day began rather hard for me and lifting the rocks facing the mountain I really found it hard and thought, how silly! What am I doing this for?

Then the sound of thunder came over the clearest blue sky. I felt the thunder on the inside of me and I knew what it meant to become a part of nature. The beauty of the group of very different people all sharing the same moment was a treasure. As we sang and walked into the chamber I knew the thunder lived inside and outside of all of us, . . . and Joseph channeled the force of beings unseen but felt.

As we stepped into the center to spread our corn on the stone and honor the four directions, the sound seemed not to belong to each individual but to the group as a whole not as a choir, rather as a single voice of the many. The wonder and clarity of each person's face was beautiful and profound as the ceremony continued. As I stepped in to the center I know that my overwhelming feeling was to offer all of what I am or could be to the Spirit, no sense of "me," just essence. And I know I could have died in that moment and been complete. In fact more complete than I could ever have imagined being. Beyond the body, beyond the mind, nothing and all in that moment.

Each direction had a subtle difference of feeling, each unformed offering of my life was met by the sound of thunder. It was a coming home that filled the soul. Pure is one of the words that comes close to that feeling, but even that does not capture the paradox of all and nothing simultaneously being manifest.

As to the wonder of the rain, and sun coming out as we finished the chant, I just know it was perfect. . . .

Rain is not simply moisture from the sky but wisdom that washes life. They say that's the blessing, that first rain. Of course, all of it is a blessing, but that was the first blessing.

Out of the eight people who participated, two never heard the thunder, as loud as it was — and it was really loud. Sometimes you can hear something, but if it's out of the supernatural, the mind blocks it out, so you don't hear it even though it is present, or else you don't remember it. The mind protects us that way.

Then it started to rain a lot, and finally I said, "OK, put your rocks down. We'll deal with them later. Let's walk over to the sound chamber." We went into the chamber. I went upstairs above the chamber and lit a cigarette. I took a puff of the cigarette and blew the tobacco smoke to the east and then to the south, to the west, to the north and then to the east again, moving clockwise. For each direction in which I blew tobacco smoke it rained more. By the time I finished the circle, it was really pouring.

There was a man there with me on the roof of the sound chamber, a lawyer from Virginia Beach, Virginia. I didn't invite him up on the roof with me; he just came along. I remember looking at him and saying, "Now, watch what happens."

I took the cigarette and walked counter-clockwise. I smoked to the east, then to the north, then to the west, then to the south. With every puff, every turn, the rain diminished. When I ended in the direction of the east, it stopped. Not even a tiny little droplet falling.

There was total, complete silence. You couldn't even hear a bird; it was that quiet. I looked at him and said, "What do you think?"

He said, "If I hadn't seen it, I wouldn't believe it."

I've never known for sure whether the spirits of my foster parents came to my dream to make it rain, or if the rain came because a Higher Intelligence honored my belief that our relatives can come and help us whenever we need help.

When I did that thunder-calling ceremony in 1991, I was following a basic pattern taught to me in the 1940s by my grandfather. The other thing he taught was to be innovative. When I was a boy with him in his kiva during the winter and I saw him walk through a wall, into a spring meadow, pick a flower, and come back, I was very impressed. I asked him, "Do you think I could do that?"

He said, "You don't want to do that, you want to do something different. I've already done that, therefore anyone can do it," meaning the villagers or whoever else wanted to could do it. "You don't need that anymore. What you need to do is something that I haven't done, something no one's done, because the whole idea is to increase the level of knowing, raise the level of consciousness."

During one of our last talks my grandfather said, "This is how far I've gotten on the potential, and your work will be to go to a higher level of potential in some areas." Some of the things I've done that he didn't do are to build peace chambers, lead sun/moon dances around the world, and speak to the

United Nations about world peace. His concentration was at the village level, and my concentration has been on the world.

When I was working in the Office of Indian Affairs in Santa Fe in 1979, a German man came in and said he belonged to a secret German society. "We're waiting for this man, and his name is Joseph. We're waiting for him because the prophecy says that when he comes, he will come from this country, from the Southwest, and he's going to be an Indian." I didn't pay any attention to it; there are a lot of Indians in the Southwest named Joseph.

Years later, my daughters said to me, "We saw a program about a prophecy. There's a man coming from the Southwest whose name is going to be Joseph, and he's going to bring some significant changes for world peace." They were concerned that it might be me because they say that in this world, what we do to peacemakers is to kill them.

I have no position at Picuris that would have been mine if I had been the leader of the Thunder Clan or my grandfather's clan. His only son, who would have taken over his responsibility at Picuris, went into the Navy during the Second World War and became a surgeon. After the war he practiced surgery in California until he retired. But although I was trained to be a Thunder-caller, I have never had a leadership position in the pueblo or the clan.

It is the same way with the Southern Ute tribe. I have led sun/moon dances for years, but never representing the Southern Ute tribe. There is no real position with the tribe that I can say is mine — that I am the leader of a particular clan or society. I think there's a reason for it. I think all of the different experiences that I had and the teachings I received from both tribes — my mother's tribe and my father's tribe — were to prepare me for something like working for the planet as a whole, to serve all of humanity

War Gods

As I was growing up at Picuris Pueblo, part of my training from the elders was to try to find the highest purpose, the highest good, for everything. I was taught to look and work for the highest good in people and in places and in things because in doing so I could achieve my highest excellence. That highest excellence, the elders taught me, was the only thing worth living for.

Once I developed that form of thinking and behavior, it became part of me. My way is to look for the highest purpose for everything, the good in everything and everyone.

I connect this teaching today to the time when I was listening to some of the Picuris storytellers talking about the people when they came from Sand Lake, from the Underworld. Because the people were afraid when they were coming from the Underworld to the Upper World, which is the world and the reality we know, they asked the War Gods to come with them. So, the War Gods came to protect and guide them.

I heard that story when I was eleven or twelve years old. One evening, about forty years later, when I was in a trance state, five spiritual beings came to ask me to go look for the War Gods that had come originally with the people from the other worlds into this world.

The five black-light beings that appeared like humans are symbolically the five vibrations of the vowels A-E-I-O-U. Additionally they represent the five right-hand fingers of Taah-meh-ney, who is the Creator-father in Tiwa mysticism.

The beings told me it was time for the War Gods to be taken home. As I received this assignment, they said I was given this responsibility because of the way that I lived, always looking for the highest good. It was now time for me to live what I had been practicing and go find the War Gods, who would either be in the Upper World, the Middle World, or the Lower World.

In a trance state, I went to the Upper World, where I found the first War God. Once he recognized me, he began to chase me. I made a hole through the top of the sky through which to re-enter this world, landing near Taos, New Mexico, at a place near my friend Joseph Rynear's house. The War God followed me, and when I landed there, he shot a ray of light at me, but I jumped and the light hit the ground where I had been standing. I then jumped over to the Sand Dunes of Colorado, and he followed me there, because he was going to capture me. As the War God came closer and closer to the Sand Dunes, the light he was emanating, which was black, began to turn white, growing clearer and purer as he neared the sand. I could see him flying toward the Sand Dunes, turning into an ever clearer light as he flew, so that by the time that he ended up where I was and fell next to me, he was so weak that the crystals of sand swallowed him. He was then taken back down into the place from which he had come.

About three years later I was visiting the Kalish Stones off the coast of Scotland with three other people. For some reason I asked them to take a rock from the place and bring it with them to the United States. Usually I didn't ask people to leave anything at a sacred place, or to take anything, like stones or pottery shards, from one. Usually I would say to leave things where they were. But this one time I asked my three companions to bring a stone with them, so each picked up a stone. The stone that I was attracted to, that I took, was very, very small, but also unusually heavy. I picked it up, put it into my carry-on bag, and later gave it to Joe Scott, from Glenwood Springs, Colorado. In a few days we were back in London and from there we flew home to the United States.

When Joe and his wife returned home two weeks later they brought with them the small, heavy stone. About a week after that, Joe asked me to come get my rock because it was blowing out their windows and doors. I was in Pennsylvania at the time. I flew to Denver and from there, with friends, drove over to Glenwood Springs to get the rock.

I realized now that the other War God was inside that rock, so I covered it in cornmeal, put it in my suitcase, and drove through the night with my companions to the Sand

Dunes of Colorado. We buried the stone there ceremonially. As we were leaving, a huge giant began chasing us. The man who was driving saw the being behind us in the dark and said, "There's a big man chasing us."

I said, "Yes, step on the gas!"

The giant chased us, but not far. In fact, he never left the sanctuary of the Sand Dunes. Apparently he was the guardian of the Dunes.

We drove to Glorieta, New Mexico, where I had some friends. That evening when we stopped, I went outside and asked for a sign or something to show me what was going on. I heard the sound of eagle-bone whistles that were used in the sun dance ceremony. That was my signal, giving me a sign that what had happened was good.

That night when I went to bed and fell into sleep, I was immediately taken to the Upper Plains where a big party was going on. Some of the people there were in ballroom dress, white gowns or tuxedos. There were also several long-bearded beings wearing colored gowns. Some were white, some red, some orange. I saw the two War Gods as they entered that level of consciousness, and one War God said to the other, "I'm glad that somebody got it because we really wanted to come home."

It wasn't long after that that the Berlin Wall came down.

I have come to believe that as we grow older, we begin to receive gifts that come from the way we see life. I am speaking of the way we care about life and carry it, and how we situate ourselves to bring us into resonance with the highest potential possibility. When we live in such a way, after a while that way rewards us.

In the years since the War God vision, there have been many local wars, but no global conflicts on the earth. I believe that we will not have a world war again because the War Gods have gone home. Interestingly, when I spoke with the War Gods they said that they were only making wars because that was what the humans wanted them to do. That was their role, the reason they had come with the people in the beginning.

The Man of Peace

FROM THE TIME I first had the vision in which an infant was planted at the center of the peace chamber in Bernalillo and I was told that this was my child to raise, I have known that he was connected to the mission of all the peace chambers and would do something important to bring about world peace. For the next eighteen years, I did my best to raise the child by teaching, doing ceremonies, and encouraging people who wanted to build peace chambers, often contributing money to help them get started. I didn't know when or how, but I figured that at some point the child would be grown and then begin to give his gifts for world peace.

In the spring of 2001, I undertook a series of ceremonies asking for knowledge about this child, and the answer that came to me during the first ceremony was a surprising one. I was told that the earthen-skinned boy I had been raising for eighteen years was myself.

All my life I had been in denial. In fact, I was given the mission to bring about world peace when I was seven, in the dream about the seven peace chambers and the grandmother weeping for joy. It was no accident that at fifteen I took part in the burial of the implements of war at Picuris. Even my connection to the Oak Ridge Boys in my forties was a sign; Oak Ridge, Tennessee, is where part of the atomic bomb was made.

Still, I only began to understand my role with world peace when the peace chamber vision came again in July, 1983. I can now admit that I must have been born a true, dyed-in-the-wool skeptic. With the second ceremony in the spring of 2001, I remembered the dream I had had at age seven and now I knew its meaning. I myself was all the aspects of my childhood dream as well, the old woman crying, the seven houses (or peace chambers). I am the seventh generation, and it has been and will be my role to work on the shamanic level for world peace.

The child is grown; the time has come.

I realized I now had the power to rid the world of warfare completely. Immediately, I did a ceremony to remove the vibrations of war from the soil and the plants on the earth — vibrations left behind from when the War Gods were here for so many millennia of human existence.

Even though I sent the War Gods back to the underworld in 1987 and prospects for peace immediately got better, wars have still been breaking out because the earth and plants still carried the War Gods' vibrations, and people, living on the earth and eating the plants, are imbued with those war energies. I removed them from the earth and the plants in the same way I might remove a disease from a person's body, using my eagle feather and my breath.

Now the environment has been purified of those ancient vibrations, and we can expect to see changes in human affairs over the next generation. While we have built war into our psyche over many centuries of warlike behavior, we will eventually not want to have war. We will seek to bring peace to our lives and to the world because the War Gods have gone home, the earth has been purified of their energies and there will be no reason for wars. We will lose our interest in them. In fact, my visions have shown me that real world peace is to come by the year 2021.

VIII. RETURNING

Being Healed

BY THE MID 1990S I was traveling most of the time, lead-ing dances in different parts of the world, but Spirit was telling me that I needed to give up the dances and turn the leadership over to my dancers. However, I didn't do what I was told. I kept traveling and leading the dances. I liked the camaraderie that comes with being with my students. After a while, every-where I went they treated me like a king. They fed me and entertained me, and I loved teaching them, even though some of those students were troublesome.

I didn't listen to the call to retire, so I started feeling sick. I went to the doctor at the Indian Health Service, and he ran tests and diagnosed me with pancreatic cancer, which is a fatal disease. People sometimes don't believe Indian Health Service doctors, but I did. I knew I was very sick.

Then I went to a medicine man who said, "Well, I'm going to do some medicine for you but you have to do what you've been told to do."

I said, "Yes." I knew then I would have to retire from leading the dances. Then, I knew also what I needed the medicine man to do for me, and I told him that.

He asked, "How do you know that's what I need to do?"

I said, "I just know. Don't argue with me. Just do it."

So, he did it. During the all-night ceremony, about three or four o'clock in the morning, I saw beings come into the room, and they sucked the malignancy out of my body. I saw actual gunk coming out of me. Then the next day I noticed a difference. In another week I started realizing a different kind of inner strength, physical strength.

I also consulted an intuitive healer, Owen James, a friend of mine from Canada. Owen gave me a protein drink. He said I needed protein, so I started taking two spoonfuls every day. I took it for maybe a month or so. That seemed to help. Also, I went to the clinic and got some vitamins. I had them do a blood test and found out that I needed some things like calcium, zinc, and multivitamins.

For about six months I was on an anti-yeast diet as well, no sugar, no alcohol of any kind, not even cough syrup, no nicotine, less red meat. It was pretty strict and I got very thin. Now I'm doing a variation of this regime. I guess it was time for me to follow my own medicine. In a way I am now building the healing center I dreamed about building at Picuris all those years ago, but the center is myself.

It has worked. When I went back to the doctor who had diagnosed me with pancreatic cancer, he discovered the cancer was gone, and he called it a miracle.

Doing What I'm Told

ABOUT THE SAME TIME I was diagnosed, in 1996, I went to see a man in the hospital in Santa Fe who was dying of cancer. His name is Ray Romero and he used to be the governor of the Pojoaque Pueblo Indians. At the time I went to see him, he had trouble with his stomach and couldn't eat any more. He hadn't eaten for thirty days.

I took some water from a pitcher that was on a table in Ray's room and used my eagle feather to sprinkle it around. Then I put water on his chest and his back. Some machine in his room started making buzzing noises and going crazy. Nobody could turn it off. I picked up my feather and said, "I'm leaving because they might think that I did something to the machine." Doctors don't really like medicine men to come in and mess with their patients, especially when they don't have permission. That afternoon Ray started eating, and he's alive today. I go see him once in a while in Pojoaque. He claims that I healed him.

People have asked me if maybe the doctor didn't make a mistake in my diagnosis, since pancreatic cancer is fatal. At this point I think that the diagnosis was right. What was even more right was my giving in to what I was told to do about my illness. Whenever I'm given something by the spiritual realm, I really need to respect it and follow it.

That's the role that mothers and fathers play with little children when they are first starting, from the time they are born until the time they are maybe seven or eight years old. What the mothers and fathers do is teach their children how to respect authority, to do what they're told. Later on they're going to have to respect the authority of the government, or of their society. Eventually, perhaps, we learn that we need to follow the authority of Spirit.

Anyhow, I finally got the message and I started taking steps to limit my involvement in the dances and turn them over to other people. At that time, I also decided to move back to the Southern Ute Reservation, to my land.

I knew that was part of what I needed to do next. I had liked living in Bernalillo, but I knew it was time and now I wasn't going to say no because I needed to pay attention, to do what I was told.

I moved in April of 1998. There had been a peace chamber on the land since the mid-eighties, and in the nineties I had started building a house above the peace chamber, mostly building it with my own hands, with help now and then from students.

All my traveling had kept me from finishing the house, and when I moved there in 1998, it was only a roughed-out frame, not yet completely weathered in. I thought that by waiting until April I could avoid the rigors of a Colorado winter in an unfinished house, but there was still some very cold weather to be endured. The freezing temperatures motivated me to work hard and finish the house, which I did over the course of the rest of that year.

The house in Bernalillo, with the original peace chamber, was rented out and then later sold. Its new owners tore down the Bernalillo peace chamber, but it still exists in crystal form in that higher plane where I saw it rise in the fork of the redwood tree.

Meanwhile, here in Colorado, remarkable things continue to happen to me. In November, 1998, about six months after my move, I went into a trance state and had a vision. I stopped breathing. I had not been sick, nor was I doing a vision quest. Sometimes I just go into trance states, and it's normal for me, but Carolyn, who had recently moved there with me, didn't know that. She checked me, found that I wa not breathing and called for help. An emergency vehicle came, and the paramedics stuck some tubes in me and took me to the hospital.

What I experienced in this trance was a vision in which I saw letters, all kinds of letters, the alphabet. There were rectangles, there were squares, forty-five-degree angles, letters, geometry and mathematics, lots of numbers happening really fast. I was told these signatures were actual experiences that I was going to have in the future.

The beings gave me a series of experiences through numbers and geometric shapes because they said that was the basis. Numbers, letters, and words form the foundation for everything in perceptual reality.

Some of my relatives, the ones who were already on the Other Side, also appeared in my vision. Someone was with them that I didn't recognize, but he seemed to be a person with some authority. He said, "No, we can't take him. He deserves to go back." So, then I was back in my body in the hospital and I was feeling those tubes they had in me.

I think I didn't die because of two things: One is that I had given people help as well as money over the years. The other was that I refrained from killing. I didn't kill even bugs. Those were the two things that kept me from leaving here.

I've always refrained from killing bugs and ants, even when they were in my house. Instead, I would ask to speak to the archetype of the bug. What were they there for? Were they in migration through my house going somewhere? There's always one main ant that I talk to about what is going on. I have to take the attitude of "live and let live." I'm not going to let them be a bothersome thing to me. If they're going to the food, then I'll just close up the food and protect it.

When I lived in Bernallilo in the trailer, ants would always come in the spring, but they were only there for maybe three weeks and then after that I wouldn't see a single ant. While they were there I would just let them run around on the counter and everything, and then they were gone.

At that point where I was ready to cross over, it came up that I didn't kill those ants. What I did, other than talking to the ant spirit, was that I took on the attitude that they had as much right to be there as I did and that I had backed my trailer house into their home one day. They were there long before I came. When I took that attitude, they were never any trouble. They would be with me for a few weeks, then I came into the house one day, and they had disappeared.

One day when I was building the house in Colorado, the telephone man was at my place, and he was talking to me while I mixed cement and put rocks in the wall for part of the foundation for the house. As we talked a chameleon kept coming up to me. I would shoo him off and he'd go maybe six or seven feet, then he'd slink back up to where I was. He wanted to communicate, and then I'd shoo him. He would go off then come back.

Finally the telephone man said, "You know that lizard loves you. He keeps coming back to you."

I said, "No, I think this is his home and I invaded it. I'm building my house on top of his."

Following My Vision

I SEE my life as a potential possibility.

Not long ago I was supposed to fly to Oklahoma to do a workshop, but a short time before I was supposed to go I found that I had no money. I figured the money would show up somehow; in this problem was the potential for something new to happen.

I normally get up around three o'clock in the morning

and go draw and paint. The day before I was supposed to fly I woke up Carolyn and said, "I have to go to the casino." I had a vision, but I didn't tell her that at first because you don't wake someone up at five o'clock in the morning and tell them that you saw a wild cherry on the slot machine. But I'd made the agreement to follow vision, and this image of the wild cherry on the slot machine kept recurring in my mind. So we went.

We got to the casino around seven in the morning, and Carolyn said, "This is totally ridiculous. I don't know what we're doing here."

"I'm going to get you a nice breakfast," I told her. "They open up at seven o'clock and they have a really inexpensive breakfast. But, you know, also, I got this vision."

I went into the casino with my last $20 and found the machine I'd seen in my vision, one of several that operate on $5 tokens. Then, I looked at another $5 machine, and I said, "Well, I'm going to put the money in that one." I did this because I was scared. What if I put my money in the machine I'd seen in the vision and I didn't win? At least if I lose on this other machine, I can justify losing. I put $5 in the wrong machine, punched it and nothing happened. I played it again and lost again. Now I only had two more $5 coins left. I decided I'd better go ahead and play the machine I'd seen in my vision. I did — and lost again. Now I had one token left, and if I lost it, I'd be completely broke. I took a deep breath, put my last $5 token in, and I hit a Wild, a 7, a Wild, for $1,200.

I like this kind of vision because it gets me out of bed.

That's just the way it is when the spiritual realm is around, and I listen to it. If I'm supposed to do something like that, the images keep reoccurring. They're subtle; they seem to happen way back in the distance, not right up front, like ideas. They're in the background, and they can sometimes be slightly annoying. It's the Universe telling me before it happens that I'm going to see something in the future.

I think life works this way. A picture is formed and it's going around a circle. Every time it reaches a certain place, it flashes back to home base. Maybe after two days or three days and it's gone around maybe five or six times, I finally get to the actual event.

Self and Vast Self

ALTHOUGH I GREW UP at Picuris, I was never an enrolled member, so I couldn't hold land there. You have to be born in Picuris to be a member. After my mother died, we needed money, so my father sold our land on the Southern Ute reservation. As a result, we ended up not having any Indian land. This land that I have my house on is an assignment.

I think, because I had no land, Spirit said, "Well, Joseph,

I'm going to make the whole world your land, so you have a home wherever you go." Sure enough, when I go to Europe, they say, "Why don't you come live over here with us?" When I go to California, they say, "We need a person like you around here. You could work at that hospital over there." And jobs, they're everywhere — people asking me to do this and that. But I'm glad to be living again on Southern Ute land.

My house and my peace chamber are on one hundred and sixty acres of tribal land which I don't own but have the right to use. In addition, the Southern Utes are giving me an elder's pension to supplement my Social Security. And, the tribe is also working on health insurance so I can go to a doctor anywhere in the world and get my bills paid.

I still travel and teach and do ceremonies and healings on occasion. People often come to see me for healings. Now I'm talking and teaching more about the spiritual realm and trying to pay more attention to "coincidences," those times when things happen unexpectedly. I'm teaching individuals and groups about how to pay attention to the spiritual realm and to follow it, because it is the basis from which the soul, the inner strength, is being nurtured. I write and draw and paint, and grow plants in a greenhouse next to my peace chamber.

That's where I've ended up. I love living out in the woods, where there are trees and land and birds, rabbits, deer, and elk. I am nurtured by being here.

It's just the way I grew up, I guess, in the wild. As a child, when I wasn't at home working, I'd be up in the mountains walking around, looking under every rock and climbing up a tree, or just watching the game, watching sunsets or sunrises, and feeling the inner peace that comes with nature.

Sometimes, as a child at Picuris, I would be sent up on the mountain to do a task-oriented ceremony. Often my grandmother would send me up to get medicinal plants. One of the things the elders always liked about me was that I would do what I was told, even though a lot of times I didn't want to.

All of that has paid off because my life now is joyful. I feel I've contributed, and I realize that there may be another request for my presence in something. When that request comes, then I'll just go do it.

The meaning of my life lies not so much in what I do, or have done, but in who I am. It is the same with all of us. We each embody the reason for our existence on this planet at this moment in planetary history. Each of us is a ceremony, a vibration of the All-That-Is. We ourselves are the Vast Self, that One Actor in the universe, who creates continually in all moments. We are the Vast Self playing in creation as creatures, as individuals.

In the experiences of my life, through loss and transformation, ceremony and story, I learned how to emerge continually from the individual self that is Joseph Earl Head Rael into the Vast Self again. In the kiva, in the sweat lodge, in the sun dances and long dances, I have learned to die to myself in order to know the Self, dying from this House of Shattering Light into states of ecstasy, and then returning again, that the Vast

Self might drink continually the light that It is creating.

To know ourselves as the Vast Self playing is to be both human and divine. It is for this we all are born, to be mystics, fully alive and dancing.